The Antichrist Is Here

The Antichrist Is Here

And The World Must Prepare

Daniel Michael Giovanni

ISBN: 1515236560
ISBN 13: 9781515236566
Library of Congress Control Number: 2015912516
CreateSpace Independent Publishing Platform
North Charleston, South Carolina

The information presented here is contained within the framework of a story, but the details are real.

CONTENTS

CHAPTER 1

THE DISCOVERY

This is nuts. I got to call Jenny.

"Jenny, did you hear?"

"No. What?"

"Uncle Jack just qualified for the US Open."

"What? That's crazy. Hasn't he been trying to do that his whole life?"

"Yup, and he just did. He's one of only nine club professionals in the entire country to make it."

"Oh man. That's insane! Where is it this year?"

"It's just outside of Tacoma, Washington on a course called Chambers Bay. Dad said he's going."

"I want to go!!"

"I know, me too. I think Mom and Dad are working on all of us going."

"All seven of us?"

"Yup."

"Oh man. That would be awesome! Wait. When does it start?"

"Next week."

"What?"

"The final qualifying is always one week before the tournament begins."

"I got to tell my boss I'm going. I'll go online to find us a house. I don't trust Dad to find a good one. What's the name of the course again?"

"Chambers Bay."

"Tell Dad he's paying the extra money for a great house."

"OK. But make sure I get my own room!"

"Yeah Yeah, I know I know me too. We can throw the boys in rooms together. Word!"

I could barely contain myself; all of us together for a week on Puget Sound in the summer; Uncle Jack playing against Tiger Woods and Phil Mickelson. Dad's going to be in his glory and Mom's going to love the break. I got to go buy some golf clothes. Wait, maybe Jenny has some good stuff in her room. I'll just borrow a few things. She won't miss them.

(Phone rings)

"What's up?"

"Are you in my room taking my stuff?"

"I'm just looking. Who told you, Dad?"

"No. I just know you."

"I don't have anything to wear."

"What? You already have a crap ton of my stuff."

"How about we just share?"

"Fine. But I'm taking my stuff back when we get home."

~

Sunday morning 4:00 came before we could blink and the limo van was in our driveway. Uncle Jack and his family were traveling with us to the airport and on the same plane out to Tacoma. All of us were excited. It's not too often that we're able to hang with our cousins. Now we'd have a whole week. This should be one for the ages.

"Jenny."

"What? I'm trying to sleep."

"Dad said that guy over there is a PGA Tour player."

"Nice. Dad should have been a PGA Tour player. Then we would have been rich."

"Be careful what you wish for. If Dad was a PGA Tour player, we might not be here. PGA Tour players are always on the road."

"Maybe. But I'm sure Mom would have been right there with him so I would take my chances."

"So the house you picked out looks real good."

"Oh yeah, I can't wait to hang out on that back deck overlooking Puget Sound sipping some wine. I'm going back to sleep so stop bugging me."

We arrived in Tacoma late in the afternoon to a beautiful summer day. What a different kind of place this is from our home in Maine; perfect summer weather, low humidity, rolling hills and pretty scenic views. We don't have anything like Mount Rainier back home. It just towers over everything. Looking around, it feels good to be with my family in a place we've never been before. My Dad and five brothers can't wait to see the course while Mom, Jenny and I can't wait for a cold glass of white wine!

The house Dad rented located just 20 minutes outside of Chambers Bay was much more beautiful than the online pictures portrayed. The magnificent hardwood floors, open spaces and leather couches were more luxurious than we were used to. Mom and Dad's master suite alone was the size of our entire downstairs back home. It included a master bath to die for, its own living room and even exercise equipment.

But the star of the house was the kitchen, oh man what a kitchen; there was enough granite counter space to host a gourmet cooking class!

A good meal and some good relaxation with a great wine and we were all off to bed. Tomorrow is a big day; Monday of US Open week and Dad is getting inside the rope access. This week will be as much his dream as Uncle Jack's, but good for him. Mom and Dad sacrificed so much to raise us seven kids. Now that we're all much older, it's high time for them to enjoy themselves.

~

As usual we were all running around on that first morning. But with the three full baths we all managed to all make it to the car on time. Except that is for me. I couldn't find my sun glasses and there was no way I was going to be stuck out on that course for 6 hours without them. Dad's beeping the horn yelling that he's not going to miss the action on the putting green for anyone and my brothers can't seem to cut me a break. Finally!

"Which one of you idiots put my sun glasses in the Kitchen junk drawer? Real nice!" I yelled in frustration.

As I went to close the drawer, an old newspaper clipping that was underneath my sun glasses moved to reveal something very strange. It looked to be some sort of notebook or journal or something. I looked a little harder and discovered it had this crazy, bizarre title, "The Final Confrontation and the Arrival of the Antichrist". The title was written on the letter head of a Catholic Church in Appleton, Wisconsin; Saint Faustina. The person's name on the letter head was that of a Father Michael Thomas. Handwritten above his name it said "My Copy." But it was the phrase written across the bottom of that top page that really caught my eye. It said, "Proof that the Antichrist is here!" What the?

I could barely contain my curiosity. I wanted to read the thing right then and there. Instead I ran downstairs and stashed it in the drawer of the night stand in my room and ran out to the Suburban with cries of "It's about time!" emanating from the mouths of every member of my family.

"Where the heck were you?" Jenny whispered.

"I've got to talk to you."

"Now what?"

"I found my sun glasses in one of the kitchen drawers and underneath them was this crazy journal thing from some Priest in Wisconsin."

"So what? Maybe he vacationed here and accidentally left it behind. Priests do take vacations you know?"

"No but it's what's written on the front of it that's insane."

"What?"

"The Final Confrontation and the Arrival of the Antichrist."

"Well maybe the guy was working on a lecture or something."

"Yeah right, and it also said, 'Proof that the Antichrist is here'. What kind of lecture is that?"

"I don't know. I'm sure it's no big deal."

"Maybe, but we got to read this stuff when we get back."

"Fine. But don't mention it to Mom or Dad. Let them have some fun this week. That's all they need is you bringing up some wacked out talk about the Antichrist while Dad is in his glory hanging out inside the ropes at The US Open watching his brother side by side with the best golfers in the world. I'm sure that would go over real big."

We arrived at the course and it was everything that we imagined. The starting times for the practice round were posted on this huge board with my uncle's name right up there with all the greatest players in the world. It was surreal. As I turned to walk up the hill a bit farther, there was my Dad already hanging out on the putting green with his brother, watching him putt along side of the who's who in golf. I didn't know all their names but I did remember seeing many of them play in the Ryder Cup just last year. It was definitely cool.

As cool as it was though, I couldn't seem to get that crazy, strange journal out of my mind. Who was this Priest, what was that bizarre title about and why would he leave something like that behind? Jenny didn't seem too willing to talk about it and my brothers were too busy trying to figure out where Tiger Woods and Phil Mickelson were. So I just had to wait until we got back to the house.

Six hours later we were all worn out, that is with the exception of my Dad who with his special family pass was inside the club house eating from a spread that would please a king. Yeah that's right. He was actually eating right alongside all the very same guys he faithfully watches on TV every Sunday. But since he was the only one from our family with that pass, none of us could go in there to get him out. So we just had to wait and wait and wait.

Eventually we made it back to the house where everyone filled their starved bodies with food; everyone that is with the exception of my Dad who was already well fed and passed out on the couch. Afterward most of us went off to take a nap; except of course for Jenny and me.

CHAPTER 2

THE JOURNAL

"Alright, show me this stuff you found."
"It's over here."

The journal had a worn look to it, like it had been used as a constant resource for years. It had a clear front cover so that the top page was visible. It was spiral bound with a black back cover. There were colored tabs and handwritten notes intermixed with printed pages and in some places a combination of all of the above on the same page. There were 167 double-sided pages in total. The only blank page we saw was the flip side of the very last page. When we opened it up and turned to the first page, a loose piece of paper fell to the floor. It was a copy of a handwritten letter.

Father Daniel Ramos
Saint John Paul II Parish
525 South 19th Street
Tacoma, WA 98465

Father Dan,

As per our phone conversation, here is the summary of the work I have gathered in my study of Eschatology and the Parousia over the last 25 years. As you know from our days back in Divinity, I started this work simply out of curiosity. But the more I uncovered, the more I realized that we are indeed living in the End Times. My efforts to propagate this information have failed thus far. Fellow priests and religious as well as the laity write it off and say that every generation has people that make these claims. My greatest fear is that this research was all for naught. Not even the faithful are prepared for what is about to happen, let alone the entire world. I hope your efforts to distribute this summary to the Bishops at the Conference will be blessed and find success. We are running out of time. The world must know and prepare!

Yours in Christ,

Father Mike.

"This is crazy." Jenny said with a stunned voice.

"I know, right? What is Eschatology and what is the Parousia?"

"Yeah, I was thinking the same thing. Let me look."

Jenny scrambled to quickly Google them on her iPhone.

"OK. I got it. Says here Eschatology is the study of the last things or of the End Times. And Parousia refers to the Second Coming of Christ."

"Man, he's talking about the end of the world." I said.

"Sure sounds like it. That's some pretty heavy stuff. I wonder who this Father Ramos is."

"It says he's from a parish right here in Tacoma. And then there's this Bishop's conference."

"Yeah just found that too. A Conference of US Catholic Bishops took place here two weeks ago at The Greater Tacoma Convention Center in Central Tacoma."

"Father Thomas must have stayed here while the conference was going on."

"Yeah but he's not a Bishop so most likely he was not in attendance."

"He was probably here to deliver his summary to this Father Ramos."

"Yeah but even still, why travel all the way out here just for that. He could have sent it overnight. There must be something else that would bring him all the way across the country. And this is his copy of all his notes. Why would he leave it here? It's obviously important to him."

"Jenny, take a look at this."

Even though we were from a religious family, nothing could have prepared us for what we read next.

"The number 333 represents the mystery of God, the Holy Trinity. The number 666 represents he who puts himself above God, Satan. "Satan's number is the key to understanding when the Antichrist (the beast) will appear.

"Revelation 13:18
'One who understands can calculate the number of the beast.'

"The reference to calculate means in part to add the number to itself. Three times since the time of Christ, Satan orchestrated an onslaught of evil upon the human race. The first began in the year 666, the second began in the year 1332 and the third and most devastating began in the year 1998.

"666 + 666 + 666 = 1998

"1998 A.D. – The Antichrist comes of age!! He is in the world right now. He is from the east, was born of a nun of Jewish descent who is a false virgin and his father was a Catholic Bishop. He is currently behind the scenes orchestrating war in the Middle East. He will soon make his entrance onto the world's stage. He will be young and good looking in appearance. He will be assisted by the False Prophet (a Roman Prince) who is currently living in the Vatican and is a Catholic Cardinal. The False Prophet will unite all of Christianity into a new one-world religion, a false church. He will then invite the Antichrist to the Vatican in Rome where he will setup his base

of operations. ('Rome will lose the faith and become the seat of the Antichrist'). When he first appears in public he will have already made his mark as a leader. He will become known as a man of peace because he will negotiate for peace but it will be a false peace. The world will marvel at his ability to accomplish peace and because of this feat, many will consider him the greatest politician that has ever lived. He will take the helm of a One World Government and a One World Religion. He will introduce a new One World currency and recommend using a high tech chip in order to implement controls for access to money, food, water and healthcare. This will be the mark of the Beast mentioned 8 times in The Book of Revelation. He and the False Prophet will work together to bring a deception so clever that few will see it coming. Through their cunning efforts, the world will be brought to its knees!"

There was stunned silence.

"So he's saying that he figured out the reference in the Bible's Book of Revelation to the number 666 and according to him, the Antichrist is in the world right now?"

"Pretty much." I said with a shocked look on my face.

"If that's true then he has solved a mystery that has stumped scholars since the time of Christ. I've watched those History Channel specials on the Book of Revelation. I've seen them discuss this 666 number. I've never heard this explanation. Most people think it had to do with the Emperor Nero."

"What? I never heard that."

"The name Nero in Hebrew and Greek translates into the number 666. He persecuted Christians not too long after the time of Jesus. But what the good Father is claiming here is light years from that."

I quickly used my iPhone to look up Revelation 13:18.

"Revelation 13:18 is just as he says and it does use the word 'calculate'."

"I guess it's possible. But how did he come up with this translation? We're in way over our heads on this stuff. Maybe we should just return the journal to the address in Wisconsin and forget about it."

"You think I should just call up there and let him know that we have his book?"

"I guess. I'm not doing it." Jenny said pulling away.

"I'll do it. Plus I'd love to ask him a few questions of my own about this stuff. I want to know if his summary was actually given to all the Bishops at the conference. That would be crazy to think that we have in our hands the actual details that were summarized in a document given to all the Bishops in the entire United States."

"Yeah I guess. It would be interesting to know if there's any truth to this stuff because if there is, this Antichrist guy can't be too far off. The Middle East is in turmoil and we did have a banking collapse. Who knows? The Antichrist could be orchestrating this whole thing. One way or another, I suspect we're going to find out."

"And then there's all this talk about a new One World Order and all that UN Agenda 21 stuff."

"Weird. Let me know if you actually get through to him. I think I'm going to take that nap now."

This is going to take some courage on my part. What do I say to him when he gets on the phone? He's going to assume I've read about his research. I'm not at all versed in this stuff. No big deal. I'll just tell him that I found his journal and ask whether I should send it back to him at the address for his Saint Faustina parish. I'm sure he'll be relieved that it's not lost. Ok here goes. Let's see, area code 414, exchange 453, ok got the last 4. It's ringing, too late to hang up now.

"Saint Faustina Church, how may I help you?"

"Hi, my name is Christina Markus. This is going to sound a little strange but I'm with my family vacationing in Tacoma, Washington and I found something that belongs to Father Michael Thomas and I was wondering if I could speak with him."

"Christina, I'm sorry but Father Michael is no longer with us."

"Oh, well do you have a forwarding address or a phone number where he can be reached?"

"Christina."

"Because as I say I have something that belongs to him and I'd liked to "

"Christina!"

"Yes?"

"Christina, Father Michael is dead."

"Oh no, what happened? Wasn't he just out here?"

"I'm sorry. All we know is that he died in Central Tacoma just two weeks ago while attending the Bishop's conference. He was found in the parking lot of Saint Leo's Church near where the conference was held, dead of an apparent heart attack. His family in Green Bay is handling all the final arrangements. I'm sorry but that's all the information I am allowed to give out."

"I'm so sorry to hear that. Thank you for your time and I'm so sorry for your loss."

"Jenny, get up!"

"What? What is it with this obsession you have with waking me up when I'm fast asleep?"

"He's dead!"

"Who's dead? What are you talking about?"

"Father Michael! I called his parish in Wisconsin and they said that he died two weeks ago right here in Tacoma!"

"What? Where? How?"

"They said he was found dead of a heart attack in the back of a Saint Leo's Church not far from the Convention Center where the conference was held."

"Man. This just keeps getting more bizarre."

"Tell me about it. I know this sounds crazy but I just can't help but feel that we should find out what happened. Something doesn't sound right."

"We don't even know him. Who would we go to?"

"I know who."

"Who?" Jenny said with a stern look on her face as if she knew what I was going to say next.

"Father Ramos."

"That's crazy. We don't know him either."

"But he's right here in Tacoma at Saint John Paul II parish."

"Think about it. What would we say to him even if we did contact him?"

"We just want to know what happened to Father Thomas. That's the least we can do."

"It's none of our business. Who do you think you are, Nancy Drew? I'm really starting to think we should just leave it alone."

I hear what she's saying, but something inside of me keeps telling me not to let this go. I just can't shake this feeling. I guess I'll pick it up again tomorrow. I'm too tired to think about this now. We have another big day ahead of us at the course and after all, this is supposed to be our vacation.

CHAPTER 3

THE MISSION

Another crisp cool day in Tacoma dawned with the usual scrambling that was part of our family routine. There was always someone that would get shut out of breakfast for trying to squeeze those last 10 minutes of sleep. And Dad was not going to tolerate any delays.

Driving to the course yielded some breathtaking views. Chambers Bay is a public golf course that was built on the site of a former sand and gravel quarry overlooking Puget Sound. Each day the Sound was filled with all different types of boats that gently showered the landscape with color and character. It was beautiful to behold.

As pretty as the sites were, the course itself was difficult to navigate. Spectators were not allowed to access key areas of the course, so our site lines were limited. But we persevered and had great fun nonetheless.

"Who's that talking with Uncle Jack?" I asked.

"Only the best, most well known sports psychologist in the entire country."

"No way; I didn't realize Uncle Jack was so well connected. Hey, take a look at Dad over there hanging around again on the putting green. He is totally eating this up."

"As they say, basking in the reflective glow."

"So are you really going to call this Father Ramos guy?" Jenny asked.

"I think we have to at least let him know that we have his friend's journal."

"I don't know. What if he doesn't want it?"

"Let's just see what he has to say."

"All right hot shot. But don't put me in the middle of it."

"Too late, you're already in the middle of it." I laughed.

Another six hours and we were all ready to head back to the house. However, this time we whisked Dad out of there before he had a chance to get lost in the club house. We were determined not to allow a repeat of yesterday. When we arrived back at the house I quickly looked up the number for Saint John Paul II parish. It was getting late in the day and I wanted to catch Father Ramos before the parish staff left for the day. Ok, here's the phone number.

"Hello, Saint John Paul."

"Hi. My name is Christina. I was looking to speak with Father Dan Ramos."

"Hold on, I'll ring his extension."

It rang several times. I was about to chicken out and hang up when just then he answered.

"Hello, this is Father Ramos."

"Hi Father Ramos," I said nervously. "My name is Christina Markus and I'm here in Tacoma with my family attending the US Open. We're renting a house here in town and I happened to come across a journal belonging to your friend, Father Michael Thomas. He must have stayed in the same house recently. I called his parish in Wisconsin to return it to him and they told me of his passing."

"Yes, very tragic."

"I'm not sure what to do with it at this point, so I thought I should give it to you."

"Christina, I'm sorry, I can't talk about this right now. But if you like, you can stop by here at the parish rectory tonight after dinner say around 7 and I can discuss this with you further. Is that OK?"

I sensed a slight panic in his voice.

"Yes that would be fine."

"Do you know where we are located?"

"Yes. I have the address. I'll use my phone for directions. My sister, Jennifer, will be with me as well."

"Very good then, we'll see you at 7."

"Ok, thank you. See you then."

Boy that was strange. He couldn't get me off the phone fast enough.

"Jenny!"

"Oh great, you've got that Nancy Drew look again, now what?"

"I talked to Father Ramos. We have to go see him at 7."

"What do you mean 'we', pale face?"

"I'm not going there alone."

"Oh yes you are. You got yourself in the middle of this thing and you can get yourself out. I'm finishing this great burger that our brother Doug just made for me and then I'm going to relax and read my book."

"C'mon."

"C'mon what? Just go over there, give him the thing and come back."

"Right, and what do I tell Dad that I need the car for by myself. At least if you're with me, we can say we're just going for a drive to see what's around."

"Oh my gosh, you're insane! Do you know that?"

"Then you'll come with me?"

"I can't believe I'm letting you manipulate me like this. Fine!"

"Ok great. We'll leave in about 2 hours."

That was easier than I thought. Usually I have to haggle with her for a good 20 minutes before she gives in. Sweet! In the mean time, I think I'll see if I can convince our brother Doug to make me one of those great burgers. US Open food just doesn't cut it.

~

"So what did you tell Dad to get the keys?" Jenny asked.

"I told him what I told you."

"And he was cool with that?"

"Yeah, he just threw me the keys."

"Either the old man is getting soft or he is absolutely having the time of his life this week and simply doesn't care anymore."

"What? I'm not going to crash the car."

"That's not the point. What happened to the 50 questions about where you're going and when you'll be back?"

"You're right. He doesn't care anymore."

"Exactly! Ok, you have to turn right up here and the Church should be on the left."

"There it is." I said. "And I guess this should be the rectory right next door?"

"Genius, it says rectory right over the top."

"Oh right. Cool. We made it."

Jenny was quick to set the agenda before going in.

"Ok, so we go in there, we say hi and we give him the book, right? None of this small talk stuff."

"Ok Ok."

The rectory was a big old converted house. It had a big front door and a door bell fit for a king. We were both a bit nervous as I pushed the button to ring the bell.

"How come the door bell doesn't play a Church tune?" I giggled.

A pleasant looking 60 something female assistant opened the door to greet us.

"Hello. May I help you?" She asked.

"Yes." I said. "We have a 7 o'clock appointment with Father Dan."

"Are you Christina?"

"Yes and this is my sister, Jennifer."

"Yes he is expecting you both. Please come in. You can have a seat here. He should be out momentarily."

"Thank you."

"Nice place, huh Jenn?"

"I love these big old houses." She said. "I will have myself one of these someday."

"Ok, here he comes."

"Hello. I'm Father Ramos. And which one of you is Christina?" He said with a smile.

"That would be me. Hello Father. And this is my sister, Jennifer."

"Jennifer, it's very nice to meet you."

"It's nice to meet you Father."

"Let's go over here into the study where there's more seating. Can I get either of you water or something?"

"No. We're good." I said.

Father Ramos looked to be an American of Mexican descent, about 50 years of age. I suspect he was born and raised here as he had no trace of any accent. He has a great smile and seems very friendly.

"Sorry to have to rush you off the phone earlier but we're all still a bit shaken about what happened to Father Mike."

"Oh, no problem."

"You can take a seat anywhere in here. So this is where Father Mike recorded all his research?" He said as I handed him the journal.

"Yes."

"Are you girls Catholic?" He asked as he began scanning some of the pages.

"Yes. We were raised Catholic and attended Catholic grammar school." I said as Jenny remained quiet.

"Are you practicing?"

"Yes. We attend Mass on Sundays, if that's what you mean."

"Are you well versed in the Faith?"

"I wouldn't say well versed but you could say we know the basics." Jenny chimed in.

"How much do you know about the circumstances of Father Mike's death?" Father asked.

"Well I was told by someone in the office at his parish in Appleton that he was out here from Wisconsin to attend the US Bishop's Conference and he had an apparent heart attack. They said that he was found in the parking lot of Saint Leo's Church. From the letter in the journal we suspect that he had given you a summary of his work to distribute to the Bishops at the conference. Is that right?"

Jenny gave me a piercing glance as if to say, "Why in the world would you tell him that?"

"Yes. I was assisting at the conference and as you say, I was working with Father Mike to have his work recognized." Father said as he handed the journal back to me.

"We've been friends since all the way back at Divinity school. He came out here to spend time with me and was hoping to address at least some of the Bishops regarding his research. The reason why I asked you to come here as opposed to speaking about it over the phone is that after Father Mike's death, I was advised by the diocese to refrain from commenting until after they complete their investigation. The circumstances surrounding his death are so mysterious that I'm actually a little paranoid that my phone calls may be in the process of being monitored."

"By whom?" I asked.

Another penetrating stare from Jenny is again sent my way.

"I don't know. All I know is that I submitted the final packet contents for review to a Cardinal Boguilegro who flew in from Rome attending as a Vatican observer and also to Bishop Walker who was the moderator for the event. Three hours later, when I began the process of placing each of the packets to the seating areas, I noticed that Father Mike's summary had been removed. I have no idea why or who may have ordered them removed."

"Cardinal Boguilegro?" I asked.

"Maybe, but I can't be sure. The day ended and I came back here, had something to eat and went straight to bed. When I awoke the next day, I was informed about Father Mike's untimely death. I know I probably shouldn't be telling you both any of this. But you see I strongly suspect that something in the contents of his journal that you found and that was summarized in the packet, has caused such a stir that someone has taken it upon themselves to completely eliminate it as though it were some kind of threat. Since you are currently in possession of the journal, I thought this was something that you both should know. The good news is that no one could possibly know that you have it. So you mustn't worry."

"Oh but we only came here to give it to you, thinking that someone more knowledgeable than us should have this for safe keeping." Jenny added.

Father's body language suddenly changed dramatically as he clearly became uncomfortable with our intentions. His reaction gave us an immediate indication of his reluctance to take possession of the journal. He pitched his head back to think while glancing up at the ceiling. The forefinger on his left hand moved back and forth across his lips. We could sense a long explanation was coming.

"Are either of you familiar with the term, The Mystical Body of Christ?"

"No not really." I said.

"The Mystical Body of Christ is the Church of which we are all members through Baptism. This Mystical Body of Christ at this time in history is moving along a similar path to that taken by the physical body of Christ from the Last Supper to the Resurrection. So just as the physical body of Christ experienced the Agony in the Garden of Gethsemane, the Scourging at the Pillar, the Crowning with Thorns, the Carrying of the Cross, the Crucifixion, the Entombment and the Resurrection, so too then will his Mystical Body, his Church, be required to suffer the same way. The two paths parallel each other. So you see, this is currently what is happening to the Church. We are under attack from just about everywhere. All you have to do is turn on the TV and watch the news and you can see that the signs are all around us. The media is relentless in reporting anything that is perceived in any way as being negative against the Church. But there are many other signs as well. And these other signs are what Father Mike discovered with his research."

"Correct me if I'm wrong, Father but if it parallels the passion and the death of Christ, then there has to be a Judas; someone on the inside set to betray his Mystical Body just as Judas betrayed him before his passion and death?"

"Yes Jennifer, excellent! That's my point. There must be a betrayal from the inside! This is precisely what Father Mike suspected was happening at the highest levels within the Church. And this is what he was exposing in both his summary and I suspect in more detail in his journal. He was trying to alert the Bishops to a monumental betrayal that he felt was imminent."

"So then if we give it to you, you will be able to expose the truth." I said.

"No Chrissy. Don't you see what he is saying?"

"No I really don't."

"He can't take the journal. Father Mike tried to expose the danger from the inside and it clearly didn't work. Father Dan also being on the inside wouldn't stand a chance. For him to attempt to expose the truth from where he sits would only result in him at best being silenced or at worst, meeting the same fate as Father Mike. And then no warning bells go off, no one is alert to the imminent danger and the faithful are left in the dark as the deception continues unabated. It can only be exposed from the outside."

"Yes. Right again, Jennifer. And now what I'm about to say to you both is something that I'm sure neither of you are prepared to hear."

Father took a deep breath, exhaled, leaned in and looked at us intently.

"I have been praying since Father Mike passed away about what to do. I did not know about this journal but I knew of his research. And now I know his work has struck a chord to such an extent that what he's uncovered must be exposed. As you say, I am powerless to make any kind of impact. I have taken a vow of obedience and so the hierarchy can choose to silence me at any time. It has happened many times in the past to those that were attempting to expose a threat to the life of the Church. Worse than that, I suspect my life would be on the line as it apparently was for Father Mike. I prayed and you called."

Father sat back, looked up to his left and gently moved his thumb and fore finger from the edges of his closed lips to their middle and back to the edges again. Deep in thought, he leaned in again.

"Children, for whatever reason, God has willed that Father Mike's life's work should fall into your hands. You have been chosen by God to reveal to the faithful and to the entire world details of a colossal deception that will befall them and of which they are completely unaware. You see, God chooses the least among us to bring his message to the world. I know this is a daunting task and probably one that you have no interest to pursue right now. You probably want to run away from this thing as fast as possible and never look back. No one would blame you if you did. But know this; if you trust in God completely, he will give you strength that you never thought possible. You will be able to move mountains. All of God's prophets were reluctant at first to accept God's call. But once they did, nothing could stop them."

There was dead silence. No one spoke for a good 20 seconds. Then Father broke the silence.

"This mission has been given to both of you. And so you must strengthen each other and pray every day asking God to guide your every step. It won't be easy but remember that you are on God's side and so you will prevail."

"But Chrissy and I don't even have a clue of where to begin."

"Christina, do you have an app on your phone that can record our conversation?" Father asked.

"Yes I do."

"Ok. Then record what I am about to say."

I fumbled through my iPhone trying to find an app I've used 100 times. All eyes were on me. My hands were shaking and I couldn't think straight.

"Ok, I got it. It's recording."

"Start here. Father Mike told me some time ago that he had uncovered the key to understanding the timetable that frames the events of our day. He said that it starts with an understanding of what happened to Pope Leo XIII on October 13, 1884."

"That's over 130 years ago."

"Yes Jennifer, that's right. On that day Pope Leo XIII was leaving the altar after celebrating daily Mass when he stopped and stood still for about 10 minutes as his face turned ashen white. He then immediately left the altar and penned the famous Prayer to Saint Michael. There were a few Cardinals along with others from the Pope's staff that witnessed this event. When he was asked what had happened, he explained that as he was leaving the altar, he heard coming from the tabernacle, 2 voices, the guttural voice of Satan and the calming, gentle voice of God. Satan was bragging to God that he could destroy his Church on earth if he were given a maximum of 100 years and more power over those who give themselves to him. Pope Leo XIII said that he then heard God respond and say, 'You have the time and you have the power. Do with them what you will.' The Pope was further made to understand that if the world turned to Saint Michael, that Saint Michael would defend them from this 100 year onslaught that Satan would inflict on the world. So in 1886, Pope Leo XIII ordered that this Prayer to Saint Michael be said after every low Mass."[1]

"What is a low Mass?" I asked.

"Before the Second Vatican Council, the Catholic Mass was called the Tridentine Mass and was celebrated by the Priest in Latin. There were two types of the Tridentine Mass, the high Mass and the low Mass. The high Mass included the playing of an organ, lots of singing, incense and in most cases more than one deacon. Think of the high Mass as being for special occasions and the low Mass as the normal everyday Mass."

"So since Vatican II, would the high Mass be considered like the Mass on Sunday and the low Mass considered the daily Mass?"

"Not exactly Jennifer but interesting that you should put it that way because that is how most apply the praying of the Prayer to Saint Michael today. Those parishes that say the prayer do designate it to be said after every daily Mass but not after every Sunday Mass. But now this is where it gets interesting. The Prayer to Saint Michael was said in all parishes around the world from 1886 until just after Vatican II completed. After 1969 with the issuing of the Novus Ordo Mass or what you might call, the New Mass, the Prayer to Saint Michael was no longer included at the end of any Mass. So for a few decades, this prayer was ignored around the world. Many point to this as being the reason why so many Catholics fell away from attendance at Sunday Mass and from the practice of the faith as a whole. The Church stopped asking Saint Michael to defend it and so they were left vulnerable to Satan's vicious plan to destroy the Church."

"But how do we know when the 100 years starts and ends?" Jenny asked.

"That's a great question. And this is what most people miss and what Father Mike figured out. In the Bible, there are a select number of books that have something to say about the end times. In the Old Testament we have the books of Ezekiel and Daniel, and in the New Testament we have certain Gospels, and letters of Saint Paul and of course the book of Revelation. In the Old Testament book of Daniel chapter 12 verse 1, we see written there:

'At that time there shall arise Michael, the great prince, guardian of your people; it shall be a time unsurpassed in distress since the nation began until that time. At that time your people shall escape, everyone who is found written in the book.'[2]

"This is a reference to Saint Michael and his role as protector of the people of God in the end times. He is then mentioned several times in the book of Revelation so we know that Michael plays a key role at the end. Father Mike posits that the 100 years that was communicated to Pope Leo XIII are the 100 years that define the end times. And that is why he was prompted to pen the Prayer to Saint Michael; precisely because this prayer fulfills this prophecy of Daniel and this prayer is the one that the faithful would use to turn to Michael for help."

"Oh. So not praying that prayer allowed Satan to advance his plan and proceed with little resistance."

"Yes, Christina. And he did make great strides during that time when the prayer was neglected. It is only recently that this prayer has made a comeback and as I said is once again being utilized in Churches around the world."

"But that still doesn't explain when the 100 years starts and ends." Jenny added.

"And that's the next piece of the puzzle that Father Mike solved. Recall that the vision of Pope Leo XIII occurred on October 13, 1884. And you might think what's in a date? But the date is the key to the mystery. When God does something, he does it at a given time and place for a reason. It's a blueprint. Most people assume that the 100 years began on the day Pope Leo had his vision. But that's not how God works. He gives the world information in advance so that they have time to prepare."

"How far in advance was the information given?" I asked.

"Let me show you. Have either of you ever heard of a place in Portugal called Fatima?"

"Oh yeah, I remember watching a movie about Fatima in Catholic grammar school." Jenny said. "Didn't Mary, the Mother of Jesus appear there to young children?"

"Yes, very well said. She appeared to three children ages 7, 9 and 10 on the thirteenth of each month for six consecutive months starting on May 13, 1917 and ending on October 13, 1917."

"So the final date of the apparitions corresponds to the date that Pope Leo XIII had his vision." I added.

"Correct. But it's what happened on the day of that final apparition in 1917 that explains the true significance of the Pope's vision. For it was on that day, that 70,000 people witnessed an event that became known as 'The Miracle of the Sun'."

"What happened?" I asked.

"For 12 minutes the sun danced in the sky while throwing off all sorts of colors onto the people and the surrounding landscape, climaxing with the sun being thrust forward as though it would fall to the earth. Most people that were there were skeptical of the apparitions until this event took place. The next day it was written about in major newspapers. For several hours before the sun revealed itself in the sky, the entire area was hit with torrential rains soaking the people. After the miracle, the ground and the people were completely dry. This was one of the greatest proven miracles in the history of the world but remarkably in our day, very few people talk about it or even know about it and yet it was less than 100 years ago."[3]

"Wow. That's crazy!" I said.

"Now, let's do the math." Father said. "How many years to the day transpired from the time Pope Leo XIII had his vision to the time 'The Miracle of the Sun' took place?"

"That would be 16 plus 17, 33." Jenny calculated.

"That's right. It was 33 years to the day! Does that number mean anything to you?"

"Not necessarily." I said.

"Not to me either."

"If you could represent God with a number, what would it be?"

"Oh ok, I see where you're going." Jenny said. "The number three is the number for God because of the Trinity. We read about that in Father Mike's journal."

"Very good, it also applies to any combination of 3 as with 33 or 333. Let me prove it to you with examples from the Bible.

- *King David is King of Israel for 40 years but his reign in Jerusalem is 33 years.*[4]
- *Jonah is in the belly of the whale for 3 days and 3 nights.*[5]
- *The 9th plague (9 is 3 3s) is 3 days of darkness.*[6]

- *Elijah proclaimed a 3 year drought on God's authority. In the 3rd year of the drought, on Mount Carmel, Elijah challenges King Ahab and his 450 prophets of Baal. He does this to demonstrate the power of the one true God in the presence of the Israelites who had been summoned by the King. 3 times he has his sacrifice doused with water before calling down fire from Heaven to consume the offering.[7]*
- *Elijah stretched himself out upon the Widow's dead child 3 times and called out to the LORD: "LORD, my God, let the life breath return to the body of this child." The LORD heard the prayer of Elijah; the life breath returned to the child's body and he lived.[8]*
- *God gives King David a choice of 3 punishments for his sin of taking an unauthorized census of Israel – 3 years of famine, 3 months of fleeing before his enemies, or 3 days of plague. King David chose the 3rd.[9]*
- *Daniel defied the order of King Darius by kneeling in prayer to give thanks to God in his upper chamber 3 times a day with the windows open toward Jerusalem.[10]*
- *Mary stayed with Elizabeth for 3 months.[11]*
- *The 3 Kings are present after the birth of Jesus.[12]*
- *Jesus is lost in the Temple for 3 days at the age of 12.[13]*
- *Jesus begins his public ministry at the age of 30 and remains in public life for 3 years.[14]*
- *Jesus institutes the Eucharist with the 3rd Cup of the 4 cups of the Passover Seder Meal, the Cup of Blessing.[15]*
- *Jesus goes off to pray 3 times in the Garden of Gethsemane as the Apostles sleep.[16]*
- *Peter denies Jesus 3 times and then later Jesus restores him by asking him 3 times 'Do you Love me?'[17]*
- *Jesus falls 3 times with the Cross.[18]*
- *There are 3 crosses on the hill of Calvary.[19]*

- *There are 3 nails on the cross.*[20]
- *The inscription over the head of Jesus, 'JESUS THE NAZOREAN, THE KING OF THE JEWS' is written in 3 languages, Hebrew, Latin and Greek.*[21]
- *Jesus is on the cross for 3 hours and dies at the hour of 3:00.*[22]
- *Jesus dies at the age of 33.*[23]
- *Jesus rises from the dead on the 3ʳᵈ day.*[24]
- *Saint Paul was struck blind for three days*[25], *was beaten 3 times with rods by the Romans, was shipwrecked 3 times*[26], *spent 3 years in Damascus*[27] *and prayed 3 times for the removal of his 'thorn in the flesh'.*[28]

And there are hundreds more references in the Bible to the number 3."

"Wow, I never noticed that before." I said.

"The bottom line is that the number 3 is code for the presence of God and those two events occurring exactly 33 years apart to the day is a sign from God that they are connected."

"So you are saying then that the 100 years that Satan requested actually started not when Pope Leo XIII received the vision, but exactly 33 years to the day later when 'The Miracle of the Sun' took place?"

"Yes, Jennifer, that's right. Because as we found out later, 'The Miracle of the Sun' was a fulfillment of the book of Revelation chapter 12 verse 1 where it states:

'A great sign appeared in the sky, a woman clothed with the sun, with the moon under her feet, and on her head a crown of twelve stars.[29]

"And this is precisely how the children at Fatima described how Mary, the Mother of Jesus, looked when she appeared to them. You see,

Revelation 12 describes a battle that takes place between this 'Woman clothed with the sun' and 'a huge red dragon'. And as verified with approved private revelation that occurred later in the century, this miracle served as an announcement to the world that the battle was now joined between these two forces."

"Wait a minute, Father. What is the huge red dragon?" I asked.

"It's Atheistic Communism."

"How do we know that?"

"Right." Jenny added. "I think I see it. I was a history major in college. Communism came into the world with the Bolshevik Revolution in Russia in early 1918."

"That's correct. The Bolshevik Revolution came just a few months after 'The Miracle of the Sun' took place in Fatima. And guess what country the Blessed Mother told the three children would become the purveyor of evil and grow to spread their errors throughout the world?"

"Russia?" I offered.

"They are and they have." Jenny insisted. "History has proven that. So if that's true, then that would mean that the 100 years are up in October of 2017!"

"Yes. Now you see the urgency and how the forces of evil must be all around us, even from within the Church, and how now more than ever they must be exposed."

Jenny and I sat there in stunned silence. Finally again Father Ramos broke the silence.

"And that's why I can't take that journal."

"So where do we go from here?" Jenny asked. "What chance do we have to bring Father Mike's research to a world oblivious of the events that are apparently about to unfold when we barely understand them ourselves?"

"You learn them. You study them hard. Then you do your own research to validate them for yourselves. And then most importantly, you pray, pray, pray and then you put your total trust in Jesus who remember is fully God. And you never forget that everything is possible with God. Attend Mass as often as you can during the week, pray the Rosary every day as well as The Chaplet of Divine Mercy especially between the hours of 3 and 4. That's the hour of mercy when Jesus died for the sins of the world. All of these will protect you from the evil one. If you don't know how to pray these prayers, I can help you. And then you tell everyone you know while keeping the instructions of our Lord in Matthew's Gospel printed firmly on your hearts as he sent his Apostles out two by two, just as he sends the two of you today.

> *'Behold, I am sending you like sheep in the midst of wolves; so be shrewd as serpents and simple as doves.'[30]*

"Learn the 7 Biblical Feasts found in the Old Testament book of Leviticus. Read about the approved apparitions that took place in 1846 in La Salette, France. Pay close attention to revelations given to the children of Fatima regarding what is known as the 'third secret'. Learn about the visions of Pope Saint Pius X. You must read Saint Faustina's Diary. Understand her connection to Pope Saint John Paul II. Read everything you can find on the apparitions of Our Blessed Mother in Garabandal, Spain in the 1960s. Focus on the events known as 'The Warning', 'The Miracle' and the 'Chastisement'. Send away for a copy of a blue book published by The Marian Movement of Priests titled, 'To The Priests Our Lady's Beloved Sons'. Read especially the entry titled, 'The End of the Times'. Read also about how Freemasonry has influenced the world and infiltrated the Church. Understand the book of Daniel's chapter 12 reference to the 'daily Sacrifice' and the 'desolating abomination' mentioned in Daniel chapters 9, 11 and 12 as well as in the Gospels of Matthew and Mark. All of this information should be detailed in Father Mike's journal because he's the one who taught me. You have everything I just revealed to you recorded. Use it as a reference. Be sure to investigate each topic one at a time. It's a puzzle but it all fits together into a cohesive picture. If you ever need my help or advice, don't send an email or call me but write to me. This way we can rest assured that our correspondence remains private."

Father sat back a third time, reading our body language as we continued to sit in stunned silence. Then he leaned in one last time.

"Listen, I understand. It's obvious you are both extremely reluctant to take this on. That's to be expected. I can assure you though that it does get better once you accept the task you have been given. Take some time and think about what this commitment might entail. It's not going to happen overnight and it doesn't have to. But the world needs to know that things are going to change and change drastically. God knows what he's doing when he makes his choices. He must see perseverance in the two of you that others don't possess. Be brave and trust in God. And please know that I will be praying for your success in this most important endeavor. Now if I may, let me extend a blessing to you for protection as you leave."

Jenny and I stood, still stunned and bowed our heads. Extending both hands over us, Father gave us his blessing.

"May the blessing of Almighty God, The Father, The Son and The Holy Spirit descend upon you and remain with you forever. Amen. Remember to ask our Lord to grant you his strength, his wisdom and his courage."

As we left we didn't even know what to say to each other. How do we possibly comprehend what we were just told? Is this real? We drove back to the house without speaking. Entering the house we went to our separate rooms with just a small glance to each other before shutting our bedroom doors.

The rest of the week was a blur. Uncle Jack didn't make the cut but we were all so proud of him. It was always a dream of my Father's to watch his brother play in the US Open and I don't think I've ever seen him as happy as he was this week. It was certainly a week for the ages and for Jenny and me that was true for more than one reason.

Jenny didn't seem to want to talk anymore about what Father had said, so I gave her some space. We'll be leaving in the morning. Maybe we can chat about it again on the plane ride home to Maine.

CHAPTER 4

FATIMA

"Ladies and gentlemen, the Captain has turned off the Fasten Seat Belt sign, and you may now move around the cabin. However we always recommend keeping your seat belt fastened while you're seated. You may now turn on your electronic devices such as calculators, CD players and laptop computers. In a few moments, the flight attendants will be passing around the cabin to offer you hot or cold drinks, as well as a light meal. We will also be showing our video presentation. Just sit back, relax, and enjoy the flight."

"Jenny, can you grab my laptop from the overhead compartment?"

"Yeah, hold on. Don't you just hate it when they pack other people's stuff in here after we get all our stuff neatly stashed? Man what a pain."

"I put it under my jacket."

"Yeah Yeah I see it."

"Thanks. I started looking up some stuff that I wanted to show you."

"So do you really believe all that stuff Father was saying about us being chosen by God to get this information out to the world? Doesn't that sound like a bit much?"

"But don't you think it's more than just a coincidence that I lost my sun glasses and then found them in the same drawer in the kitchen, where it just so happens, Father Mike left his journal? The thing was under a newspaper in the back of the drawer and the only reason I saw it was because I was moving stuff around trying to find the glasses."

"I guess I'm just not as gullible as you."

"But you seemed to be getting into it when you talked about all that history stuff."

"Yeah that actually all made sense to me and it did match up pretty well with the actual history."

"Here, look at this. These are actual photos I downloaded of 'The Miracle of the Sun' at Fatima on October 13, 1917. Look at all these people looking up."

"Wow, that's crazy. How could all these people have seen this miracle and yet nobody talks about it? I never hear Priests bringing this up in their sermons. You would think they would use this kind of thing to get people inspired about the faith. This is the kind of stuff that would convince a ton of people that what the Church teaches is actually real and this is proof. You can't fake this."

"Yeah I know. Did you know that the children were shown a vision of Hell?"

"What?"

"Yeah, I'm serious. Listen to what the oldest child Lucia wrote years later about what they saw."

"Our Lady showed us a great sea of fire which seemed to be under the earth. Plunged in this fire were demons and souls in human form, like transparent burning embers, all blackened or burnished bronze, floating about in the conflagration, now raised into the air by the flames that issued from within themselves together with great clouds of smoke, now falling back on every side like sparks in a huge fire, without weight or equilibrium, and amid shrieks and

groans of pain and despair, which horrified us and made us tremble with fear. The demons could be distinguished by their terrifying and repellent likeness to frightful and unknown animals, all black and transparent. This vision lasted but an instant. How can we ever be grateful enough to our kind heavenly Mother, who had already prepared us by promising, in the first Apparition, to take us to Heaven. Otherwise, I think we would have died of fear and terror."[31]

"Yikes!"

"I know, right?"

"People need to hear that." Jenny insisted.

"I know. Most people don't even believe that Hell is real. But these kids saw it. And then they were given this prayer to pray to help keep people from ending up there. See if you recognize it."

"O my Jesus, forgive us, save us from the fire of hell. Lead all souls to Heaven, especially those who are most in need."[32]

"Oh yeah, I remember saying that when we prayed the Rosary at Saint Martha's. What's it called again?"

"It's called The Fatima Prayer."

"Well that makes sense."

"And then here's what the Mother of Jesus told them about what was coming in their future."

"You have seen hell where the souls of poor sinners go. To save them, God wishes to establish in the world devotion to my Immaculate Heart. If what I say to you is done, many souls will be saved and there will be peace. The war is going to end: but if people do not cease

offending God, a worse one will break out during the Pontificate of Pius XI. When you see a night illumined by an unknown light, know that this is the great sign given you by God that he is about to punish the world for its crimes, by means of war, famine, and persecutions of the Church and of the Holy Father.

"To prevent this, I shall come to ask for the consecration of Russia to my Immaculate Heart, and the Communion of reparation on the First Saturdays. If my requests are heeded, Russia will be converted, and there will be peace; if not, she will spread her errors throughout the world, causing wars and persecutions of the Church. The good will be martyred; the Holy Father will have much to suffer; various nations will be annihilated. In the end, my Immaculate Heart will triumph. The Holy Father will consecrate Russia to me, and she shall be converted, and a period of peace will be granted to the world."[33]

"When did you have the time to find all this stuff?" Jenny asked.

"I've been researching it like Father said to do. That's what I've been doing these last few days when we weren't at the course. I could tell that you didn't want to talk about it so I didn't bother you. So let me ask you. You know history. When she says that the war is going to end, I'm assuming she means World War I?"

"Yes. World War I was still going on in 1917, but it was coming to an end. But what is more interesting to me is what she says after that about a worse one coming during the Pontificate of Pius XI if people do not stop offending God."

"Well that would be World War II."

"Right but she's telling them this long before it happens and even names the Pope that will be around at that time. That's incredible!"

"I also pulled down the list of Popes for the last 200 years."

"Perfect! Who was Pope in 1917 when the apparitions took place?"

"That would be Benedict XV. He was Pope from 1914 until 1922."

"And then who came after that?"

"Oh. It was Pius XI; the one that she names."

"So there was no Pius XI when she told them that. And he was Pope until when?"

"Until 1939."

"Until when in 1939?"

"Um. Ok, it says here that he died on February 10, 1939. Does that match up with history?"

"Well most people trace the start of World War II to when Hitler invaded Poland in September of 1939. But actually Hitler's first move was when he annexed Austria in March of 1938 when Pius XI was still Pope. So technically what she said is absolutely correct. That first move was really what raised the curtain on World War II."

Jenny thought a little more and then continued.

"And then what about that line about a night illumined by an unknown light? I wonder what that means. Do you have Father Mike's journal handy? Have you been looking at it?"

"Oh yeah, I have it in the overhead. Do you want to grab my carry-on?"

"Yeah, hold on. Does he say anything about it?"

"Not sure. We'll have to look at it together."

"Pull down that tray thing."

"Ok." I said. "He talks about Fatima right in the beginning so if he mentions anything about it, it should be here in this first section somewhere."

"Look for that quote."

We fumbled through the journal like it was a competition to see who could find it first.

"There Chrissy! Read item #6."

There was a list in the journal on page 7 that summarized all the key points of Fatima and sure enough item #6 referenced this unknown light.

"The Mother of Jesus told Lucia that when you see a night illumined by an unknown light know that it is a sign from God that the world is about to be punished by means of a war worse than WWI. On the night of January 25 and the early morning hours of January 26, 1938, the arroyo borealis was seen as far south as southern Italy. It was the first time the arroyo had been seen like this since 1709. Lucia sees it from her convent window in Tui, Portugal and knows immediately what it means. The next day papers from all over the world wrote about it. 47 days later, Hitler invaded Austria."[34]

"Wow! Look and he even has the actual newspaper clipping from The New York Times for January 26, 1938."

- The New York Times January 26, 1938
  - "London, January 25th, 1938. The Aurora Borealis rarely seen in Southern or Western Europe spread fear in parts of Portugal and lower Austria tonight while thousands of Britons were brought running into the streets in wonderment. The ruddy glow led many to think half the city was ablaze. The Windsor Fire Department was called out thinking that Windsor Castle was afire. The lights were clearly seen in Italy, Spain, and even Gibraltar. The glow bathing snow-clad mountain tops in Austria and Switzerland was a beautiful sight but firemen turned

out to chase non-existent fires. Portuguese villagers rushed in fright from their homes fearing the end of the world."

- "Grenoble, France, January 25th, 1938. A huge blood-red beam of light which scientists said was an Aurora Borealis of exceptional amplitude tied up telephone systems in parts of France tonight and spread anxiety in numerous Swiss Alpine villages. Emblazoned in the Northern sky the light brought thousands of telephone calls to Swiss and French authorities asking whether it was a Fire? War? or the End of the World?"

I could see Jenny's frustration building.

"Why doesn't anyone talk about this? Incredible events took place in 1938 just as the children were told 20 years earlier. And then all of these messages were validated with probably the most visual miracle ever recorded, The Miracle of the Sun, witnessed by 70,000 people! Why isn't this shouted from every pulpit in the world?"

"I don't know; maybe because it was intentionally suppressed." I said.

"This is crazy. People all over the world have been looking for proof of God's existence and it's been right there in front of them the whole time! How frustrating is that?"

Jenny's enthusiasm took her from a skeptic to an apostle in about an hour's time. It was great to see. I need a partner in crime or far from an exposure; this information will just wind up in another drawer somewhere.

"But Jenny there's a whole other part to what the children were told. And that hasn't unfolded yet."

"Right, all that stuff about Russia and its connection to Communism. And once again it was predicted before it happened. I mean can any reasonable person argue that Russia and Communism were not the biggest propagators of evil around the world then and now?

"And look what Russia just did in the Ukraine. It's pretty obvious that the consecration of Russia that she asked for must not have been accomplished."

"Yeah what is that consecration stuff all about? See if there's anything in the journal about that."

"Actually it's #3 in his list. Here look at this."

"The Mother of Jesus told the children that she would return to request the Consecration of Russia to her Immaculate Heart and if done it would bring peace to the world. But if not, Russia would spread her errors throughout the world causing wars and persecutions. As promised the Blessed Mother did return to Lucia to ask for the consecration of Russia to the Immaculate Heart of Mary in order to forestall the coming war. This happened on June 13, 1929. She told Lucia that the time had come for her to go to the Holy Father and request that he consecrate Russia to her Immaculate Heart in union with all the Bishops of the world. She said that if this was done it would avert the coming conflict and there would be peace. If not, Russia would continue to spread her errors throughout the world and God would punish the world for its sins by means of war and persecution of the Holy Father.

"Sister Lucia mentioned in her memoirs that the Consecration of Russia must be done by the Pope in union with all of the Bishops of the World and Russia must be specifically mentioned. Sister Lucia did get an audience with the Pope and she did communicate Mary's wishes but for whatever reason Pope Pius XI did not do as

*the Blessed Mother requested. Years later Sister Lucia would write
in her memoirs that because that was not done, so much evil came
into the world that could have been avoided."[35]*

"Why in the world would the Pope and the Bishops not perform the
consecration right there in 1929? How hard could that have been? It
would have avoided World War II and maybe even The Depression."

"The Pope must not have believed Lucia." I said.

"But there were 70,000 people who just witnessed The Miracle of
the Sun not 12 years prior. How did that not validate everything that
Lucia was saying?"

"It does make you wonder what they were thinking. Look at what
the journal says next."

*"In the summer of 1931, Sister Lucia was sent by her religious superior
to Rianjo, a small city in Spain. While she was there, she went to the little
church of Our Lady of Guadalupe where she prayed for the conversion
of Russia, Spain and Portugal. While there, Jesus spoke to her and said:*

*'Make it known to my ministers, given that they follow the example
of the King of France in delaying the execution of my command
(to consecrate Russia), they will follow him into misfortune. It will
never be too late to have recourse to Jesus and Mary.'*

*"When Jesus refers to 'My ministers' he's referring to the Church
hierarchy. In 1689, exactly 100 years before the French Revolution,
Jesus requested that the King of France consecrate France to his Sacred
Heart. The king also did not do as requested and hence The French
Revolution in 1789 devastated France.[36][37] Now apply that to today
and consider that the Consecration of Russia to the Immaculate Heart*

of Mary that was requested over and over again, still has not been done; and here we are now almost that same 100 years later. This does not bode well for the Church hierarchy in our time."

"So let me get this straight. In 1917 there were prophecies validated by the most incredible miracle known to man, and those prophecies were ignored. Then subsequent requests made from Heaven through this same visionary directed at the hierarchy of the Church in both 1929 and 1931 that could have changed the course of world events for the better were also ignored? I thought that the hierarchy were the good guys and in tune with Heaven. How could they have missed all this?"

"I'm really not sure, Jenn, unless as I said before there were those in the highest levels within the Church that even then were already working to suppress it. But look at this. It says here in the journal that the Fatima apparitions were officially approved by the Bishop of Fatima just 13 years later in October of 1930."[38]

These facts frustrated Jenny even further.

"That means that by the summer of 1931 when Jesus issued his warning to the hierarchy of his Church, Fatima had already been approved. What were they afraid of?"

"I don't know. It doesn't make sense. Ok, so after Pope Pius XI, Pope Pius XII was elected Pope in 1939 and it says that he did perform the consecration not once but twice; once in 1942 and then again 10 years later in 1952."[39]

"Why did he do it twice?"

"It says that in 1946 Sister Lucia agreed to an interview and explained that the consecration performed by Pope Pius XII in 1942 did not satisfy the requirements because it did not specifically mention Russia and not all the Bishops participated."[40]

"So he had to perform it again?"

"Right. In 1952 he performed the consecration again and he did mention Russia this time but once again it wasn't done in union with all the Bishops of the world. Get this, apparently no one told the Pope about that second requirement regarding the Bishops even though Lucia specifically stated it in her memoirs."[41]

"You can't make this stuff up." Jenny said in her continued frustration.

"Guess what?"

"Now What?"

"It doesn't end there."

"What doesn't end there?"

"On May 13, 1982, Pope John Paul II went to Fatima exactly one year after being shot and he also performed a consecration. But the consecration did not mention Russia and once again the world's Bishops did not participate."[42]

"What is it with these Bishops?"

"I don't know. So in March of 1983 Sister Lucia told Pope John Paul II's representative to Portugal that the 1982 consecration once again was not sufficient because it did not specifically mention Russia and the Bishops did not participate. So the Pope performed yet another one this time in Rome on March 25, 1984. He had the Fatima statue flown over to the Vatican for the ceremony."[43]

"Did it work?"

"Wait, the notes get a little confusing here."

I had to pause to read ahead.

"Oh I see."

"See what?"

"Remember that blue book that Father Ramos mentioned?"

"Yeah I think so."

"It's called, 'To The Priests Our Lady's Beloved Sons'. Apparently that book is filled with messages from the Mother of Jesus to an Italian Priest starting in 1973 and ending in 1997. What Father Mike says here in his journal is that this Priest was given a message on the same day that Pope John Paul II did this second consecration, March 25, 1984. In that message, this Priest was told specifically that the Pope sent letters in advance to every one of his Bishops and invited them to perform the consecration in union with him on that day."

"Did they have to be there in Rome with him?"

"No. They just had to pray in union with him at that time from wherever they were."

"Well did they all do it?"

"Nope, the message says that not all the Bishops welcomed the invitation and so the explicit consecration of Russia was not done according to her request."[44] [45]

"Oh man, how many times is the Catholic hierarchy going to disobey a direct request from Heaven? This is proof that there must have been intentional resistance to Fatima among the hierarchy starting all the way back to 1917 and continuing on even until today."

"Yeah, I agree. Now listen close to this. This Priest was also told in that same message that the Consecration of Russia to the Immaculate Heart of Mary will eventually be done according to her original request but not until the bloody events are well underway."[46]

"And that's why, Chrissy, understanding all of this is so important to us today because it has everything to do with what's still going to happen."

"Yup, and that's what Father Mike emphasizes in his journal."

"Wait, were the children at Fatima told about bloody events?"

"Yeah, don't you remember this?"

"If my requests are heeded, Russia will be converted, and there will be peace; if not, she will spread her errors throughout the world, causing wars and persecutions of the Church. The good will be martyred; the Holy Father will have much to suffer; various nations will be annihilated. In the end, my Immaculate Heart will triumph. The Holy Father will consecrate Russia to me, and she shall be converted, and a period of peace will be granted to the world."

"Oh man! That's what's going to happen now."

"Or very soon." I said.

"Did she actually use the word annihilated?"

"That's crazy that you should ask that."

"Why?"

"Because look here. Father Mike actually addresses the use of that word and the notion of Russia being a world power. Listen to what he says."

"People laughed at the children when they identified Russia as the country in need of conversion because in 1917 Russia was a poor, religious nation on the point of collapse. They were far from a military, political or even economic power and certainly did not have the capability to annihilate a nation. And yet Lucia was adamant that it was Russia that the Blessed Mother identified and it was the word 'annihilated' that she used."

"And so the Bolshevik Revolution came to Russia in 1918 and the rest is history. And here is Russia today taking Ukraine and then threatening the rest of the world by reminding them that they have nuclear weapons while Europe and the US implement devastating sanctions on Russia. It's like backing an angry animal into a corner. They'll strike back in any way they can."

"Actually Father Mike does refer to Russia as the 'Bear' that is mentioned several times in the Bible."

"That sounds about right."

"Amazing isn't it?" I said. "The message of Fatima is playing out right in front of our eyes and no one knows."

"And then there's that 100 year thing."

"What do you mean?" I asked.

"I mean that whole thing with France in 1689 that we just read. Jesus told the king of France in 1689 to consecrate France to his Sacred Heart and the king ignored his request. And exactly 100 years later came The French Revolution. The king of France, Louie XVI was beheaded and 1000 years of monarchy came to an end. He was the only king of France ever to be executed. So now look at the 100 years that Pope Leo XIII heard Satan bragging about and how we now know it's connected to Fatima and another consecration that is requested over and over again, this time a consecration of Russia, and just like the king of France the hierarchy of the Church fails to do as instructed. And in 1931 Jesus tells Lucia to remind his ministers and warn them what happened in France when the King ignored his request. Can it be any clearer what's going to happen?"

"And we're about to come to the end of the 100 years. History is repeating itself!"

"But this time when the fallout comes, it will fall directly on the hierarchy and even the Pope. Remember?"

"If my requests are heeded, Russia will be converted, and there will be peace; if not, she will spread her errors throughout the world, causing wars and persecutions of the Church. The good will be martyred; the Holy Father will have much to suffer;"

"It all fits together. Remember what Father Ramos said about the parallels between the suffering of the physical Body of Christ and his Mystical Body, the Church? Now the only question becomes …."

"I know what you're going to say, which Pope?"

"Exactly."

"Does Father Mike address that in the journal?"

Once again I had to scramble to read ahead.

"Oh man, oh man, oh man!"

"What?"

"Yes he does. Listen to this. When the apparitions at Fatima took place, the Pope was Benedict XV."

"Right we already talked about that."

"I know but now he's talking about the Pope right before Benedict XV, Pope Pius X. In 1909 and then again right before he died in August of 1914, he had visions that involved a future Pope in the end times. This is what Pius X said that he saw in the first vision."

"'What I have seen is terrifying!' he cried out. 'Will I be the one, or will it be a successor? What is certain is that the Pope will leave Rome and, in leaving the Vatican, he will have to pass over the dead bodies of his priests!'"[47]

"And this is what he said he saw in the second vision."

"I have seen one of my successors, of the same name, who was fleeing over the bodies of his brethren. He will take refuge in some hiding place; but after a brief respite, he will die a cruel death. Respect for God has disappeared from human hearts. They wish to efface even God's memory. This perversity is nothing less than the beginning of the last days of the world."[48]

"So I bet that this is what The Blessed Mother was referring to when she told the children that the Holy Father will have much to suffer."

"Right, and what Father Mike is saying here in the journal is that this vision solves the puzzle of which Pope will have much to suffer."

"You mean where Pius X says 'of the same name'?"

"Yes, but listen to how Father Mike solves the puzzle."

"The visions of Pope Saint Pius X identifies exactly who the Pope is that will have much to suffer. When he says 'one of my successors, of the same name', most people automatically assume that he's talking about his assumed name of Pius. But neither Pius XI nor Pius XII that came after him had any such experience. And because he makes reference to the end times, that puts us squarely into our time because of the other reasons I have already stated. So then what does Pius X mean? He is referring to his actual name. Pope Pius X's actual name was Giuseppe Sarto. Giuseppe in Italian means Joseph. Pope Benedict XVI's actual name is Joseph Ratzinger, the same first name as Pope Pius X. The Pope that will have much to suffer is Pope Benedict XVI."[49]

"Wow! If that's true Chrissy, then he must also be the one that finally performs the consecration of Russia. I wonder if he knows all this."

"I'd bet he does."

"It's just so crazy that all of this is about to unfold and people in general are clueless."

"I know. And think of this." I said. "There was a Pope Benedict at the start of the apparitions at Fatima and at the start of the 100 years of Satan's assault. And now, as the 100 years are about to expire and the crucial Fatima messages are about to be fulfilled, we have the next Pope Benedict, yet another connection to Fatima. Is that a coincidence or a sign?"

"Who knows? But what is sure is that we are quickly coming down to the wire."

"I guess now we can understand why Father Mike was so determined to expose this truth. People need to know and they need to prepare."

"But Chrissy, let's be clear about what this means and why the fulfillment of these prophecies will affect everyone in the entire world. If the 'Huge Red Dragon' is Atheistic Communism with Russia as its kingpin, and if it's making this one final push to completely dominate the world, then not just Russia will be involved. It must also involve China, the biggest communist country in the world. And that will mean nothing short of World War III."

Jenny and I spent the rest of the flight trying to comprehend all that we had discovered, but still completely stumped as to how we could possibly make a difference and expose these truths to a world so thoroughly in the dark. That dilemma would have to be left for the days, weeks and months to follow. For now we were content with continuing our efforts unraveling the events that were sure to materialize in the near future.

CHAPTER 5

THE THIRD SECRET

Be it ever so humble and you know the rest. It felt good to be back in Maine after all we had done. Jenny and I committed to continue working together putting the pieces to a puzzle together that we had absolutely no idea where it would take us. We were both very intrigued by what we had found so far and the thought that we may have been given the secrets that unravel future events that have stumped many a scholar was as much overwhelming as it was thrilling. And so we pressed on.

"Jenny, are you on your way home?"

"Yeah, I'll be pulling up in about 2 minutes."

"You're not going to believe what I just found. If you think that it was baffling how some in the hierarchy of the Church were intentionally obstructing the Consecration of Russia, you haven't heard anything yet."

"What do you mean?"

"Remember how Father Ramos told us to look into what he called, 'The Third Secret of Fatima'?"

"Yes."

"Ok, so the first two secrets were the vision of Hell and the prophecies surrounding World War II."

"Right."

"But this third secret has everything to do with what is still to come."

"What is it?"

"Ok, hurry in and I'll show you the whole thing."

"I'm coming in now."

I heard Mom and Dad asking each other what Jenny and I were up to. I suspect that we won't be able to keep this under wraps much longer.

"What did you find?" Jenny asked as she burst into the room and jumped on the bed.

"Ok, so in October of 1943 the Bishop of Fatima sends Sister Lucia a formal letter to write down what is called the Third Secret of Fatima. Apparently it was well known that there were 3 parts to the secrets that were revealed to the children. But when Lucia tried to write it down, she found it too difficult to do probably because it was too devastating to think about. So get this, on January 2, 1944, Mary the Mother of Jesus again appears to Lucia and tells her that she must write down this third part of the secret and that it needs to be revealed to the world no later than 1960. So she writes it down and has it delivered to the Bishop of Fatima by her spiritual director on June 17 of that same year with the instructions regarding 1960. In April of 1957, it is finally delivered to the Vatican and put in a safe where the Pope lives. On August 17, 1959, the Pope at the time, Pope John XXIII, reads it and decides that it is not for his time. He has it put back in the safe and does not reveal it in 1960 as The Blessed Mother specifically requested! Can you believe that?"[50]

"Unbelievable."

"Now many of the Catholics around the world had heard about the fact that this secret was supposed to be revealed in 1960 so people were waiting anxiously to hear what it said. Even the media got into it. But nothing was given. It was a major disappointment."

"I can't believe we've never heard about any of this. That wasn't even that long ago."

"I know."

"Well do we know now what the third secret is?"

"This is what is known. In 1952, the Pope at the time, Pope Pius XII, sent a priest to question Sister Lucia about the third secret. He was told by Lucia that this third secret had two parts to it. The first part had to do with the Pope and the other part he said had to do with the completing of the sentence, '*In Portugal the dogma of the faith will always be preserved.*'[51] So the thinking is that it would follow logically then that this second part must refer to the fact that outside of Portugal, meaning in most of the rest of the world, the dogma of the faith will not always be preserved."

"Right, so there will be a falling away from the Faith."

"Yes and Father Mike's journal references these end time scriptural passages about this very thing."

2 Thessalonians 2:1
"*Let no one deceive you by any means; for that day will not come unless the falling away comes first, and the man of sin is revealed, the son of perdition.*"

1 Timothy 4:1
"*Now the Spirit explicitly says that in the last times some will turn away from the faith by paying attention to deceitful spirits and demonic instructions.*"

Matthew 24:5
"*For many will come in my name, saying, 'I am the Messiah,' and they will deceive many.*"

Matthew 24:9-11
"*Then they will hand you over to persecution, and they will kill you. You will be hated by all nations because of my name. And then*

many will be led into sin; they will betray and hate one another. Many false prophets will arise and deceive many."

Matthew 24:25
"False messiahs and false prophets will arise, and they will perform signs and wonders so great as to deceive, if that were possible, even the elect."

2 Timothy 4:3
"For the time will come when people will not tolerate sound doctrine but, following their own desires and insatiable curiosity, will accumulate teachers and will stop listening to the truth and will be diverted to myths."

Luke 18:21
"When the Son of man comes, will he find faith on the earth?"

John 16:2
"They will expel you from the synagogues; in fact, the hour is coming when everyone who kills you will think he is offering worship to God. They will do this because they have not known either the Father or me."

"I also read that in 1984, long before he was Pope Benedict XVI, Joseph Ratzinger gave an interview where he said that the things contained in the third secret have already been announced in Sacred Scripture."[52]

"It all fits together doesn't it?"

"Yes it does." I said.

"And boy, doesn't that last passage from Scripture remind you exactly of what's happening right now with Muslim Extremism? Because did you know that Islam denies the existence of the Trinity?"

"No I did not. That makes the passage even more precise because it says they will kill the faithful and claim to be doing it for God. Incredible, isn't it, that Jesus said those words 2000 years ago and yet it appears to be happening right now."

"By the way," I said, "Pope Benedict XVI himself in May of 2010 told the press that the third secret reveals that this falling away comes from attacks not just from outside the Church but that the greatest persecution will come from inside the Church itself."[53]

"That must be why some in the hierarchy worked so hard to suppress the revealing of this secret because it exposes them."

"Yeah, I was thinking the same thing."

"But what do we know about the first part of the third secret?"

"Ok, that part was finally revealed on June 26, 2000. Here, I'll read it to you."

"… at the left of Our Lady and a little above, we saw an Angel with a flaming sword in his left hand; flashing, it gave out flames that looked as though they would set the world on fire; but they died out in contact with the splendour that Our Lady radiated towards him from her right hand: pointing to the earth with his right hand, the Angel cried out in a loud voice: 'Penance, Penance, Penance!'. And we saw in an immense light that is God: 'something similar to how people appear in a mirror when they pass in front of it' a Bishop dressed in White 'we had the impression that it was the Holy Father'. Other Bishops, Priests, men and women Religious going up a steep mountain, at the top of which there was a big Cross of rough-hewn trunks as of a cork-tree with the bark; before reaching there the Holy Father passed through a big city half in ruins and half trembling with halting step, afflicted with pain and sorrow, he prayed for the souls of the corpses he met on his way;

having reached the top of the mountain, on his knees at the foot of the big Cross he was killed by a group of soldiers who fired bullets and arrows at him, and in the same way there died one after another the other Bishops, Priests, men and women Religious, and various lay people of different ranks and positions. Beneath the two arms of the Cross there were two Angels each with a crystal aspersorium in his hand, in which they gathered up the blood of the Martyrs and with it sprinkled the souls that were making their way to God."[54]

"Wait a minute!" Jenny said.

"What?"

"That sounds exactly like the visions of Pope Pius X."

I paused for a second to consider the impact of what she was saying.

"You're right! I didn't pick up on that before. That can't be a coincidence. They have to be connected."

"And the visions of Pius X were received just a few years before the apparitions at Fatima."

"So, all of these visions occurred in the same basic time period."

"This even further confirms the claim that Pope Benedict XVI is the Pope spoken of by the children at Fatima that has much to suffer. The first part of the third secret is a perfect match to Pope Pius X's visions which we know now identifies Pope Benedict XVI through his first name, Joseph. This is amazing! Hasn't anyone put this together before? It's kind of obvious wouldn't you say?"

"I would." I said. "And I guess that's what Father Mike was trying to demonstrate, that all these things are connected."

"Did the Vatican claim in 2000 that this was the entire secret?"

"Yes and that's when all the controversy erupts regarding this third secret. The official line is that this is the entirety of the secret and oh by the way, it refers to Pope John Paul II's assassination and not something in the future."

"That's nonsense. It doesn't take a genius to figure out that the first part of the secret clearly states that the Pope in the vision is killed, not shot and wounded. They must think we can't read and comprehend the words."

"Not only that but it refers to the Pope passing through a city half in ruins littered with corpses. That was clearly not the case when Pope John Paul II was shot."

"This is just their way of saying, 'there's nothing to see here, move along' and washing their hands of the entire matter. They look like fools though because even a surface study of the facts reveals what you found, that the third secret is in two parts and one of them refers to a great falling away from the faith. This is confirmed by Pope Benedict XVI himself."

"Right, but Pope Benedict XVI not only said that but as recently as five years ago on May 13, 2010, the 93rd anniversary of the first apparition at Fatima, he said this."

"Whoever thinks that the prophetic mission of Fatima is concluded deceives himself."[55]

"Ok Chrissy, this is what I have so far. Tell me whether I have this right. The third secret of Fatima is in two parts. The first part we have word for word and we know it actually refers to Pope Benedict XVI and not Pope John Paul II. The second part of the secret refers to a great falling away from the faith except in Portugal where it will be preserved. And the greatest part of the falling away will begin from inside the Church itself. Do I have all that correct?"

"Yes. That is consistent with everything I have found."

"Ok so now we need to figure out what exactly it is that will change from inside the Church that will cause this great falling away. Because all indications are that it will spread from there and then out to the rest of the world. Have you checked Father Mike's journal to see if he provided any details about how this will transpire?"

"Yes. And I think I've already identified it. Remember that blue book published by The Marian Movement of Priests 'To The Priests Our Lady's Beloved Sons' that I mentioned before and Father Ramos told us that we needed to send away for?"

"Yeah, of course."

"Well, I sent away for it and it arrived today."

"No way, let me see it."

I handed Jenny a 970 page soft cover book in a bright blue casing, with a picture of the statue of Our Lady of Fatima and Father Stefano Gobbi a humble Italian priest on its front cover. The book is filled with what are known as interior locutions received by this humble priest. I learned that an interior locution refers to the reception of supernatural messages from Heaven based on an inner knowing. It is not received from an audible voice or a vision. Individuals that receive these types of messages often describe it as hearing the voice from within their sole, interiorly.

Through this humble priest, an organization called The Marian Movement of Priests was formed on October 13, 1972. There's that Fatima date again. Pope John Paul II gave this organization his Papal Blessing and the movement has received an official approval from the Roman Catholic Church stating that this literary work is totally free from error in all matters of faith and doctrine. This I found out is called an imprimatur.

The book displays each message that was received by Father Gobbi in chronological order starting with the first locution dated July 7, 1973 and ending with the last locution dated December 31, 1997. In total there are 604 messages that are detailed in the book.

⁓

"Oh man, there are hundreds of messages in here." Jenny observed.

"I know."

"And each one of these is a message from Mary the Mother of Jesus to this Italian priest?"

"Yup."

"And the Catholic Church was cool with all this?"

"Pope John Paul II gave the movement his official Papal Blessing which is a really big deal. He also would frequently invite Father Gobbi to the Vatican to meet with him privately to discuss the messages he was receiving. If you look towards the back of the book, you will see pictures of Father Gobbi with Pope John Paul II."

"So does Father Mike's journal make reference to any messages in this blue book that confirm this great falling away from the faith begins from inside the Church?"

"Yes it does."

"Does it tell us what's responsible for this great loss of faith?"

"I suspect it does but I haven't found that part yet."

"Well come on, let's see if we can figure it out!"

"Right, but before we go there, I need to show you the messages that tell us exactly what the second part of the third secret says."

"Ok, so stop smiling and tell me!"

"Ok ok. There's a lot here so be patient. Here are excerpts from 4 messages found in the blue book regarding the Third Secret of Fatima."

Message #362, September 15, 1987, Akita, Japan (Feast of Our Lady of Sorrows)

(Paragraph h) "I am weeping because the Church is continuing along the road of division, of loss of the true faith, of apostasy and of errors

which are being spread more and more without anyone offering opposition to them. Even now, that which I predicted at Fatima and that which I have revealed here in the third message confided to a little daughter of mine is in the process of being accomplished. And so, even for the Church the moment of its great trial has come, because the man of iniquity will establish himself within it and the abomination of desolation will enter into the holy temple of God."

Message #406, June 13, 1989, Como, Italy (Anniversary of the Second Apparition at Fatima)

(Paragraph g) "The black beast like a leopard indicates Freemasonry; the beast with the two horns like a lamb indicates Freemasonry infiltrated into the interior of the Church, that is to say, ecclesiastical Masonry, which has spread especially among the members of the hierarchy. This Masonic infiltration, in the interior of the Church, was already foretold to you by me at Fatima, when I announced to you that Satan would enter in even to the summit of the Church. If the task of Masonry is to lead souls to perdition, bringing them to the worship of false divinities, the task of ecclesiastical Masonry on the other hand is that of destroying Christ and his Church, building a new idol, namely a false christ and a false church."

(Paragraph l) "Thus errors are spread in every part of the Catholic Church itself. Because of the spread of these errors, many are moving away today from the true faith, bringing to fulfillment the prophecy which was given to you by me at Fatima: 'The times will come when many will lose the true faith.' The loss of faith is apostasy. Ecclesiastical Masonry works, in a subtle and diabolical way, to lead all into apostasy."

Message #425, May 13, 1990, Fatima, Portugal (Anniversary of the First Apparition at Fatima)

(Paragraphs g, h, i) "My third secret, which I revealed here to three little children to whom I appeared and which up to the present has not yet been revealed to you, will be made manifest to all by the very occurrence of the events.

"The Church will know the hour of its greatest apostasy. The man of iniquity will penetrate into its interior and will sit in the very temple of God, while the little remnant which will remain faithful will be subjected to the greatest trials and persecutions.

"Humanity will live through the moment of its greatest chastisement and thus will be made ready to receive the Lord Jesus who will return to you in glory."

Message #489, March 15, 1993, Fatima, Portugal

(Paragraphs d, e, f) "I have wanted you here, because you must communicate to all that as of now — as of this year — you have entered into the events which I foretold to you, and which are contained in the third part of the secret, which has not yet been revealed to you. This will now be made evident by the very events themselves which are about to take place in the Church and in the world.

"My Church will be shaken by the violent wind of apostasy and unbelief, as he who sets himself against Christ will enter into its interior, thus bringing to fulfillment the horrible abomination which has been prophesied to you in Holy Scripture.

"Humanity will know the bloody hour of its chastisement; it will be stricken with the scourge of epidemics, of hunger and of fire; much

blood will be spilt upon your roads; war will spread everywhere, bringing down upon the world incommensurable devastation."

"Wow!" Jenny said with a slow whisper. "That's why the second part of the secret was suppressed. They didn't want anyone to know that the culprits would be found within the Church hierarchy."

"Yeah, I know. It's crazy, right?"

"So this 'man of iniquity' guy, he's the …"

"Antichrist!" I blurted out.

"And he gets to the summit of the Church? Does Father Mike's journal confirm this?"

"Yes it does."

"And what about the prophecies in Holy Scripture that are mentioned in these messages about this guy? Does the journal go into those?"

"Yes it does."

2 Thessalonians 2:3

"*Let no one deceive you in any way. For unless the apostasy comes first and the lawless one is revealed,* the one doomed to perdition, who opposes and exalts himself above every so-called god and object of worship, so as to seat himself in the temple of God,* claiming that he is a god— do you not recall that while I was still with you I told you these things? And now you know what is restraining,* that he may be revealed in his time. For the mystery of lawlessness is already at work. But the one who restrains is to do so only for the present, until he is removed from the scene. And then the lawless one will be revealed, whom the Lord [Jesus] will kill with the breath of his mouth and render powerless by the manifestation of his coming, the one whose coming springs from the power of Satan in every mighty* *deed and in signs and wonders that lie, and in every wicked deceit for those who are perishing because they have not accepted the love of truth so that they may be saved."*

Matthew 24:15
"So when you see the abomination of desolation spoken of by the prophet Daniel, standing in the holy place (let the reader understand), then those in Judea must flee to the mountains,"

Daniel 7:25
"He shall speak words against the Most High, and shall wear out the saints of the Most High, and shall think to change the times and the law; and they shall be given into his hand for a time, times, and half a time."

Daniel 8:23
"At the end of their reign, when sinners have reached their measure, there shall arise a king, impudent, and skilled in intrigue. He shall be strong and powerful, bring about fearful ruin, and succeed in his undertaking. He shall destroy powerful peoples; his cunning shall be against the holy ones, his treacherous conduct shall succeed. He shall be proud of heart and destroy many by stealth. But when he rises against the Prince of princes, he shall be broken without a hand being raised."

Daniel 11:36
"The king shall do as he wills, exalting himself and making himself greater than any god; he shall utter dreadful blasphemies against the God of gods. He shall prosper only till the wrath is finished, for what is determined must take place. He shall have no regard for

the gods of his ancestors or for the one in whom women delight; for no god shall he have regard, because he shall make himself greater than all. Instead, he shall give glory to the god of strongholds; a god unknown to his ancestors he shall glorify with gold, silver, precious stones, and other treasures. He shall act for those who fortify strongholds, a people of a foreign god, whom he has recognized. He shall greatly honor them; he shall make them rule over the many and distribute the land as a reward."

"And so this is the guy that the elusive second part of the Third Secret of Fatima was warning about and who will deceive the faithful to fall away from the true faith. And Father Mike really says that this is the guy that's about to come front and center in a clueless world within the next few years?"

"That's what he says." I said. "But it's not just him that sent out warning signals about the coming of the Antichrist and everything that comes along with him. Listen to what Pope John Paul II himself said just 2 years before he became Pope."

"We are now standing in the face of the greatest historical confrontation humanity has ever experienced. I do not think the wide circle of the American Society, or the wide circle of the Christian Community realize this fully. We are now facing the final confrontation between the Church and the anti-church, between the Gospel and the anti-gospel, between Christ and the Antichrist. This confrontation lies within the plans of Divine Providence. It is, therefore, in God's Plan, and it must be a trial which the Church must take up, and face courageously...

"We must prepare ourselves to suffer great trials before long, such as will demand of us a disposition to give up even life, and

a total dedication to Christ and for Christ. With your and my prayers, it is possible to mitigate the coming tribulation, but it is no longer possible to avert it, because only thus can the Church be effectually renewed. How many times has the renewal of the Church sprung from the shedding of blood? This time too, it will not be otherwise. We must be strong and prepared and trust in Christ and in his Holy Mother and be very, very assiduous in praying the holy rosary."[56]

"All this information is available and still no one sees what's coming because the information has been intentionally suppressed." Jenny says out of frustration. "So the world doesn't know what it doesn't know and yet it's about to get slammed in the face by a title wave of deception that it's completely unprepared to comprehend let alone defend against."

"I guess that's why only a small remnant is left to stand and fight."

"Sitting ducks, that's what we are!"

"There's just one last thing that I found about the Third Secret of Fatima that I have to tell you. If you think you were frustrated before by how at every step along the way certain members of the hierarchy of the Church blocked the successful consecration of Russia and then suppressed the all important third secret from being fully revealed, get this. Guess what they did to Sister Lucia as she tried time after time after time to accomplish what The Blessed Mother had requested both with the consecration and the third secret?"

"Don't tell me they shut her down."

"Yup, they silenced her! When the Church made clear in 1960 that it was not going to reveal the contents of the third secret, the press went to see Sister Lucia to get her comments and they found that she had been silenced by the Vatican. So she was not able to speak about it again publicly."[57]

"Unbelievable. The primary visionary of an approved apparition that was validated by probably the greatest miracle since the resurrection of Jesus 2000 years ago, and who had information that could have changed the course of events in the world for the better if only she had been listened to and taken seriously, is shut down by the very Church itself. Where were the good guys in all of this? How did they let the few bad guys get the upper hand?"

"It's inconceivable."

"Remember how I pointed out to Father Ramos that there had to be a Judas, a betrayal from the inside if in fact as he said that the Church as the Mystical Body of Christ is traveling the same path that the physical Body of Christ took to the Cross?"

"Yeah, that was a pretty brilliant observation on your part. I remember he was impressed."

"Well, here's your Judas moment, a flat out betrayal from the inside."

"And from what we've learned so far, that betrayal will only continue."

"Yeah, because how could this Antichrist guy possibly ascend to the summit of the Church if he is not welcomed in by the powers that be?"

"He can't." I said.

"Well that makes one thing crystal clear."

"What's that?"

"Father Ramos was right. If they could silence Sister Lucia, then he would have been shut down in a heartbeat. He would have had no chance exposing these truths."

"So maybe it really is left to us. Maybe it really is us against the world."

"I'm starting to believe it is, and for the first time I actually feel that it's God's will that we expose this. I just can't stand the thought of these guys getting the upper hand and deceiving the entire world. With

God's help and the help of his remnant we have to take it to them. They won't even see us coming. They'll be blindsided."

"Amen to that, Jenny! Now you're talking."

"You know what we need?"

"What's that?"

"We need a prayer that will be our calling card; something condensed and powerful that we and everyone we come in contact with can all get behind to pray, Jew and Christian alike."

"Wait, I think I have one. In Father Mike's journal, he closes each chapter with this prayer. How about we adopt the same one? "

"Let's see it."

"Ok, here it is."

"Eternal God, in whom mercy is endless and the treasury of compassion inexhaustible, look kindly upon us and increase Your mercy in us, that in difficult moments we might not despair nor become despondent, but with great confidence submit ourselves to Your holy will, which is Love and Mercy itself. Amen."[58]

"That's perfect! Let's make sure we say it often and pass it on to as many as we can."

CHAPTER 6

THE ABOMINATION OF DESOLATION

There's not much better than life in the summertime at our seaside home in Old Orchard Beach. This is a special place and we know it. Jenny and I would often retreat to the expanse of our pristine beaches to escape the typical bustle of activity found in a home with 7 children. It offered us the calm required for productive study. With this as a backdrop, on this crisp, sunny, July beach day, we made our most significant discovery to date.

"Have you taken a good look at this blue book and the span of years that the messages run?" Jenny asked hinting that she already knew the answer."

"No but I'm guessing you have."

"Well, look at this. The first message was received by Father Gobbi on July 7, 1973 and the last one was received on December 31, 1997."

"Ok, so the total span of the messages ran about 24 ½ years."

"Right and the average number of messages per year numbered about 25."

"That sounds about right. But what's your point?"

"The very last message was received on December 31, 1997."

"Yeah I know, you already said that."

"That doesn't sound any alarms for you?"

"No not really."

"Remember that day when we first opened up the journal and you just happened to open it up to a page that told us something important about a particular year."

"Yes, yes, it was 1998. Father Mike indicated that it was significant because it was the sum of 666+666+666. And he said it was a key indicator that the Antichrist was not just in the world but had come of age and would soon become very active behind the scenes of world events."

"Well don't you think that it's more than just a coincidence that the last message received by Father Gobbi came just hours before the clock turned to 1998? After 24 ½ consecutive years and an average of 25 messages per year, more than a few of which warn about the coming of the Antichrist and then nothing, nothing else, everything stops."

"Wow! That's an incredible observation. I suspect that it's not an accident."

"No. That's by design."

"Well if that's true, then he could have a hand in the world's continuing economic struggles and the spreading of wars everywhere."

"I would say that's highly likely given what we have learned." Jenny said.

"Man, it's like a crescendo building and building until it reaches this final confrontation."

"Right, the final confrontation; and that's exactly where we're headed."

"But what's still so perplexing is this fast approaching apostasy, this great falling away from the faith that we know is coming. What could possibly cause it to accelerate to a point where almost all are deceived?"

"There must be a trigger, Chrissy, an event of such magnitude that it causes a mass exodus from the true faith and into a colossal error."

"As I said before, I suspect it's in here somewhere but I just haven't found it yet."

"I couldn't help but notice in those last messages we read from the blue book about the third secret, and then again in the Scripture readings, references to what Father Ramos insisted that we needed to pay close attention to and understand; an 'abomination of desolation' also referred to as the 'horrible abomination'. That sounds pretty colossal. What does that mean?"

"Well I just took it to mean the thing that results when the Antichrist enters into the Church."

"That could be but why would that alone make it desolate? To make something desolate you need to first empty it."

"The journal does talk about a one world religion that the Antichrist will control."

"Well that must be where the deception comes in. How could you pull that off without getting people to change what they believe? He does say that even the Catholic Church gets sucked into it, right?"

"Yes he does." I said.

"Ok, so are there any references he uses from the blue book that could explain how they pull this off?"

"There is this one that he keeps referring to over and over again. But I haven't had a chance to study it yet. It's message #485."

The message was titled "The End of the Times" and in 3 ½ pages it summarized the entire sequence of what was to come. It was like nothing we had read previously. It spoke of precisely what we were looking for, an explanation of what the Bible calls the "abomination of desolation", the "horrible abomination" and the "horrible sacrilege".

"Wait Jenny, this message was mentioned by Father Ramos by name as something once again where we needed to focus attention. And reading into it, this must be the order that everything happens. It describes first the spread of errors and then the outbreak of wars. After that comes the bloody persecution of the faithful."

"This whole thing is going to be much more difficult than we thought. Look there Chrissy, start reading from paragraph 'o'."

Message #485, December 31, 1992, Vicenza, Italy

(Paragraphs o, p)

"The fourth sign is the horrible sacrilege, perpetrated by him who sets himself against Christ, that is, the Antichrist. He will enter into the holy temple of God and will sit on his throne and have himself adored as God.

"'This one will oppose and exalt himself against everything that men adore and call God. The lawless one will come by the power of Satan, with all the force of false miracles and pretended wonders. He will make use of every kind of wicked deception, in order to work harm.' (2Thes 2:4, 9-10)"[59]

"That last paragraph is right from one of the scripture passages that we read just a little while ago, the one from 2 Thessalonians chapter 2."

"That's right. I thought that sounded familiar. Ok, keep reading."

(Paragraph q)

"'One day, you will see in the holy place he who commits the horrible sacrilege. The prophet Daniel spoke of this. Let the reader seek to understand.' (Mt 24:15)"

"And that one is from Matthew 24:15 which we also just read. But this is a slightly different translation." Jenny astutely observed. "This one uses the words 'horrible sacrilege' where the translation that we read previously uses the words 'abomination of desolation'."

"So that would have to mean then that they represent the same phenomenon."

"Right and that phenomenon I bet is what causes the great falling away. Let's read on."

(Paragraphs r, s)

"Beloved children, in order to understand in what this horrible sacrilege consists, read what has been predicted by the prophet Daniel: 'Go, Daniel; these words are to remain secret and sealed until the end time. Many will be cleansed, made white and upright, but the wicked will persist in doing wrong. Not one of the wicked will understand these things, but the wise will comprehend.'

'Now, from the moment that the daily Sacrifice is abolished and the horrible abomination is set up, there shall be one thousand two hundred and ninety days. Blessed is he who waits with patience and attains one thousand three hundred and thirty five days.' (Dn 12:9-12)"

"So now we see yet another variation on the same phenomenon, the term 'horrible abomination'. And it appears to be connected to what the prophet Daniel calls the abolishing of the 'daily Sacrifice'."

"Wait." I said. "Remember when we were with Father Ramos he also stressed that we needed to understand the reference in the book of Daniel to the 'daily Sacrifice'. This is what he was talking about. He also talked about this phenomenon and referred to it as the 'desolating abomination' which once again is a slightly different way of referring to the same thing. He even gave us all the places in the Bible where it's referenced. I want to look those up real quick so we know what they are. He said Daniel 9, 11, 12 and in the Gospels of Matthew and Mark. Daniel 12 and Matthew 24 are two that we already covered. Here are the remaining ones from Mark 13 and Daniel 9 and 11."

Mark 13:14
"When you see the desolating abomination standing where he should not (let the reader understand), then those in Judea must flee to the mountains, [and] a person on a housetop must not go down or enter to get anything out of his house, and a person in a field must not return to get his cloak."

Daniel 9:27
"For one week he shall make a firm covenant with the many; half the week he shall abolish sacrifice and offering; in their place shall be the desolating abomination until the ruin that is decreed is poured out upon the desolator."

Daniel 11:31
"Armed forces shall rise at his command and defile the sanctuary stronghold, abolishing the daily sacrifice and setting up the desolating abomination."

"So the 'desolating abomination', 'the abomination of desolation', 'the horrible abomination' and the 'horrible sacrilege' are all terms that are used in the Bible to refer to the same thing. And now we know that they are all connected with the abolishing of the 'daily Sacrifice'. Now we just need figure out what the 'daily Sacrifice' refers to."

"And then what causes it to be abolished?" I said.

"I suspect if we continue reading the message, we will find the answers. I can see it already in that next sentence."

(Paragraphs r, s)

"The Holy Mass is the daily Sacrifice, the pure oblation which is offered to the Lord everywhere, from the rising of the sun to its going down.

"The Sacrifice of the Mass renews that which was accomplished by Jesus on Calvary. By accepting the Protestant doctrine, people will hold that the Mass is not a sacrifice but only a sacred meal, that is to say, a remembrance of that which Jesus did at his Last Supper. And thus, the celebration of Holy Mass will be suppressed. In this abolition of the daily Sacrifice consists the horrible sacrilege accomplished by the Antichrist, which will last about three and a half years, namely, one thousand two hundred and ninety days."

"And there it is, Chrissy, exactly what we were looking for."

"So the Catholic Mass is the 'daily Sacrifice' that the Bible is referencing in all these Scripture passages?"

"Haven't you ever heard the Mass referred to as 'The Holy Sacrifice of the Mass?"

"Wow, that's right! So the hierarchy is going to officially change the essence of what the Mass is!"

"That's what it says. They are going to officially accept the Protestant doctrine from the days of the Protestant Reformation which dates all the way back to the year 1517. We studied the Reformation in World History."

"And this will cause the great falling away?"

"Yes, and won't last longer than 3 ½ years or 1,290 days. This makes total sense because as we said before, in order to create a one world religion, you would need to deceive a very large group of people to accept changes to what they currently believe. It looks like it's going to be the Catholics. If the essence of the Mass is changed to what the Protestant Churches already believe, then you can bring all of Christianity under one belief system. It's brilliant in its deception because it would tug at the heart strings of every Catholic to love your neighbor. And so the hierarchy could propose it as offering a small compromise for the sake of Christian unification. People would go for that. But what they wouldn't realize is that actually they would be accepting something that amounts to an earthquake to the authentic Catholic faith."

"Right," I said, "because most Catholics are completely unaware of what the Catholic Church really teaches about the Mass, so making a compromise like this will seem like a minor change and overall a good thing."

"As I say; a brilliant disguise."

"Hey, look at this. There's a section in the journal right after where this message is first referenced, where it gives a detailed explanation as to how it is that the Catholic Mass is the 'daily Sacrifice' that the Bible is referring to."

> "When we attend MASS, the perfect Sacrifice that Jesus made for sin on the cross is re-presented to God the Father for our sins. The Catechism of the Catholic Church says in paragraph 1366 where it quotes the Council of Trent:
>
> '[Christ], our Lord and God, was once and for all to offer himself to God the Father by his death on the altar of the cross, to accomplish there an everlasting redemption. But because his priesthood was not to end with his death, at the Last Supper 'on the night when he was betrayed,' [he wanted] to leave to his beloved spouse the Church a visible sacrifice (as the nature of man demands) by which the bloody sacrifice which he was to accomplish once for all on the cross would be re-presented, its memory perpetuated until the end of the world,

and its salutary power be applied to the forgiveness of the sins we daily commit.'

"Through the power of the Priesthood, the Priest brings the Living Presence of Jesus, Body, Blood, Soul and Divinity to us on the Altar under the appearance of bread and wine. And then all of us present in the Church, as a congregation, re-present Jesus and his once-for-all Perfect Sacrifice made on Calvary to God the Father, and apply its power to the forgiveness of the sins that we commit on a daily basis!

"Once this offering is accomplished, we then bind ourselves to it in Holy Communion by receiving Jesus in the Holy Eucharist, Body, Blood, Soul and Divinity and allowing his Precious Blood to wash over us and cover us. Remember that this part of the Mass is called The Liturgy of the Eucharist and its foundation comes directly from the Old Testament Passover. Recall that Jesus was celebrating The Seder Meal of The Passover at The Last Supper when he transformed the "natural" elements of the Passover meal, the bread and wine, into the "supernatural" presence of The Lamb of God, Jesus himself truly present, Body, Blood, Soul and Divinity and then soon after offered himself on the Cross to God The Father for the sins of the world. This is why Jesus is both truly Priest and Victim. The Priest saying the Mass takes the place of Christ the Priest; 'in persona Christi' meaning in the person of Christ, but Christ the Victim remains the same!

"So just as at the very first Passover the Israelites sacrificed a lamb, offered it to God, roasted its flesh, covered the doorpost of their homes with its blood and received the flesh of the lamb so that when death came to their door, death would pass over their home, they would be freed from the slavery of the Egyptians and taken to the Promised Land; so too we then present the once for all perfect

sacrifice of the Lamb of God, Jesus, to God The Father, receive him Body, Blood, Soul and Divinity and cover ourselves with his precious blood so that when death comes to us, death will pass over us, we are freed from the slavery of sin and taken to the Promised Land of Heaven!

"Do you see how Jesus transforms the 'natural' elements of the Passover into his 'supernatural' presence in the Mass and then the incredible power it has? So the Mass is like a lightning bolt through all of Salvation History.

"Also remember that the perfect Sacrifice that Jesus made is the only perfect Sacrifice available to the human race. Therefore it is the only acceptable offering that we have that makes perfect reparation to God the Father for our sins. Once again, when and where do we do this? We do this during the 'Holy Sacrifice of the Mass'. Nowhere else is the living presence of Jesus made available to us for the very purpose of allowing us the opportunity to offer perfect reparation to God, the Father, for our sins and the sins of the whole world.

"So if the hierarchy of the Catholic Church officially changes the essence of the Mass from a re-presenting of the actual once-for-all perfect Sacrifice of Jesus on Calvary to God the Father for the sins of the world, to simply a remembrance of the last supper in the upper room, it would usher in a tsunami of consequences since it would mean then that nowhere would the required perfect reparation be offered to God the Father for sin.

"Most Christians (Catholics and Protestants) are oblivious to what the Catholic Mass truly represents. This is why even some Christian Scripture scholars completely miss the meaning of the Bible references to the abolishing of the 'daily Sacrifice'. And yet it is the key to unraveling the mystery of the end times. Most think it refers to Old Testament sacrifices. But these ended millennia *ago. Yet the Holy Sacrifice of the Mass is offered every day in every corner of the world almost nonstop for the sins of the world, and yet very few recognize it as such. The Holy Sacrifice of the Mass is Sacred Scripture's 'daily Sacrifice' that will be abolished by the hierarchy of the Catholic Church. The individual that signs off on this catastrophic change will be The Biblical False Prophet! This will pave the way for the Antichrist to enter into the interior of the Church since the true Lamb of God will no longer be present in the tabernacles of Catholic Churches around the world, thus making them desolate. This absence will establish 'The Abomination of Desolation'."*

"That's absolutely amazing but it makes total sense that the Antichrist will only be able to establish himself within the heart of the Church when Jesus is no longer present there to stop him. His road block will be removed when they change the Mass."

"And I bet, Jenny, the changes will be so subtle that most of the faithful won't even pick up on it. Most will just go along because they won't want to rock the boat."

"Except for the remnant who will and they will stand in direct opposition to these changes. And many will be martyred because of it."

"Wow! Remember that day when we first opened the journal and read about how it will be the work of the False Prophet that will establish the new One World Religion that will enable the Antichrist to set up his base of operations in Rome? Well, now we know that he will accomplish this by changing the Catholic Mass to make it acceptable to all Protestant faiths. But I'm still curious as to how exactly he will pull this off. I'm sure there will be fierce opposition to any such efforts."

"I would hope so. Either way we're going to find out."

"Well when he does, then we'll know who he is, and we can expose him."

"Be careful what you wish for."

"Why, I'm not afraid."

"Oh believe me, if all these things come to pass as predicted, you will be."

"Then let's pray fervently, pleading for God's help. And let's repeat it often."

"Eternal God, in whom mercy is endless and the treasury of compassion inexhaustible, look kindly upon us and increase Your mercy in us, that in difficult moments we might not despair nor become despondent, but with great confidence submit ourselves to Your holy will, which is Love and Mercy itself. Amen."

CHAPTER 7

THE WARNING

I love Sunday mornings but this one was particularly crisp with a slight chill in the air that held the buzz as each family member slowly went through their morning routine to start this magnificent day.   I'm always the first one up and love sipping my coffee from the confines of our comfortable umbrella covered outdoor couch. In the cool quiet of our multi-colored stone patio, I take great delight observing our home from afar as it comes to life. This particular morning I was filled with excitement as if it were Christmas morning, waiting for Jenny to wake. We had uncovered so much about the end times in such a short period of time that I couldn't wait to discover more.

"Wake up sleepy head."

"Chrissy, leave me alone and let me sleep." Jenny said speaking into her pillow.

Knowing full well it wouldn't curtail my efforts to wake her; she rubbed her head unable to think of a way to put me off a little longer so she could claim ten more minutes of sleep.

"I was so wiped out from working on all that stuff we figured out on the beach. What Mass are we going to?"

"Mom and Dad said they're going to the 11:30 and I think the boys are going too. Let's just go with them."

"Sounds good, it'll give me a chance to eat some breakfast."

"No eating inside an hour before Mass!"

"I know, I know. Hopefully something's already made."

"Actually, there is. Mom made a ton of scrambled eggs and there's still some turkey bacon left."

"Nice."

"By the way, I happened to overhear Mom and Dad talking and trying to figure out what we've been working on. They were laughing that whatever it was, at least we were not fighting."

"Oh, I'm sure that's coming at some point."

"Well their guesses didn't even come close."

"Yeah right, like their actually gonna guess, 'Hey, I think they might be working on when the Antichrist is going to appear'."

"Yeah I know." I said cracking up with laughter.

"Hey, before I fell asleep last night, I was thinking about that place in Spain that Father Ramos mentioned that we needed to learn about. It was kind of a long name but I remember that I'd never heard of it before. When I did my 6 months as an exchange student in Italy I traveled all around Europe. My friends and I spent a few days in Spain. We loved it there. But I never heard of this place that he mentioned. Do you remember the name? I wanted to look it up and see where in Spain it was."

"I remember him mentioning Spain but I can't remember the name. Go eat your breakfast and I'll listen to my iPhone recording again."

"Yeah sounds good."

I did remember Father Ramos mentioning Spain and that there were apparitions of The Blessed Mother there so I studied the recording I did.

"Let's go guys." Mom yelled. "We're gonna be late!"

We all piled into the Suburban with the boys in the back and of course Jenny and me in the middle seat.

"Garabandal." I whispered to Jenny.

"What's Garabandal?"

"That's the place in Spain!"

"Oh, oh, right. I want to see if I can find it on my phone. I'm just curious where it is exactly. Spell it."

"G-A-R-A-B-A-N-D-A-L."

"Oh ok, it's in a mountain range in Northern Spain. And it's actually called San Sebastian de Garabandal."

"When you were in Spain, where did you go?"

"Mostly in and around Barcelona, that's all the way on the east coast of Spain, close to southern France."

"So Garabandal was far from where you were."

"Oh yeah, from looking at the map, I would say it's about 500 miles away. But here's something interesting."

"What's that?"

"It says here that it's only about 450 miles away from Fatima."

"But that's in Portugal."

"Right but Portugal borders Spain. But that's not all. It also says that there's another very famous apparition site of The Blessed Mother in Lourdes, France. And that also is only about 450 miles away."

"Wow, so all three of these famous apparitions took place in generally the same part of Europe?"

"That's right. That's got to say something."

"It's probably because the faith is so strong in those areas."

"That would make sense. Well, when we get back, I want to dive in and learn about what happened in Garabandal."

"Yeah me too."

"Ok guys, let's go, I want to get into the Church before the Mass starts." Dad announced as we pulled into our parking space.

This Mass would turn out to be different from any other. About half-way through the Mass, I glanced over at Jenny and there were tears rolling down her face as she was staring at what appeared to be the big cross mounted high above the tabernacle. I couldn't get her attention to find out what was wrong. After a few minutes she bowed her head and began wiping her tears. I tried to say something to her but she shook her head as if to say "not now". The rest of the Mass went as normal. As we exited the Church and we all got back into the Suburban, Jenny remained quiet, still not wanting to talk. When we arrived back home she went right to her room and gently closed the door. Not wanting to intrude, I left her alone until she was ready to talk. Three hours later as I was continuing my study of the journal, there was a knock on my door and then Jenny walked in.

"What happened back at the Mass?"

"I almost can't explain it. As we were kneeling during the Eucharistic prayer and as the Priest said the blessing and then lifted the host, I saw a brilliant light emanating from the host that I had never seen before and then I felt the most loving voice speaking within me, inside of me. It was like the voice was speaking throughout my entire life and throughout my entire being."

"Oh my gosh!"

"I looked around and I realized that no one else was experiencing what I was. I knew immediately that the voice was that of Jesus and he said to me, 'My child, do not be afraid. I AM with you. Trust in Me.' I could feel his love permeate through me. It was like nothing I had ever experienced before. It made me weep for joy. Afterward I needed to quietly reflect on what had happened. That's why I went off on my own. It was made clear to me but not through words that people need to know that these are the end times and they must return to God. What we're discovering will come to pass. Things will become very difficult as the world is purified in preparation for the return of Jesus."

We both sat in quiet reflection, contemplating what this meant. Suddenly our work was far more important than we had comprehended previously. This was proof that God was indeed counting on us to bring his message to the entire world. It was overwhelming. We knelt and prayed the Rosary together. Afterward, we knew we must persevere in our studies.

~

"Ok, since returning from Mass, I've been studying up on the apparitions at Garabandal. Father Mike's journal has an entire section devoted to what happened there. So let me just read you his summary."

"Starting on July 2, 1961 in a small town in Spain called Garabandal; Mary the Mother of Jesus appears once again this time with dire warnings for the future. She appears to 4 girls, 1 is age 11, and the other 3 are age 12. The primary visionary is Conchita Gonzalez.

"In the evening of June 18, 1961, the four girls were playing on the outskirts of the town when suddenly they heard a loud noise, like thunder, and saw before them the bright figure of the Archangel Michael. On the following days the Archangel appeared to them again in the same place. He announced that on July 2, Mary the Mother of Jesus would appear to them.

"On Sunday, July 2 at 6PM the 4 girls went to the place where the Angel had appeared and sure enough Mary appeared to the children while accompanied by two angels, one of which was St. Michael. This is their description of what they saw:

'She is dressed in a white robe with a blue mantle and a crown of golden stars. Her hands are slender. There is a brown scapular on her right arm, except when she carried the Child Jesus in her arms.

Her hair, deep nut-brown, is parted in the center. Her face is long, with a fine nose. Her mouth is very pretty with lips a bit thin. She looks like a girl of eighteen. She is rather tall. There is no voice like hers. No woman is just like her, either in the voice or the face or anything else.

'At times they said the wind rustled her long hair which reached down to her waist. The girls spoke with the Virgin with the utmost naturalness. 'We were telling her,' they said, 'about our tasks, how we were going to the meadows...' and 'she smiled at the little things we told her.' She showed them how to treat her: 'Like children who speak with their mother and tell her everything...Children who rejoice to see her when they have not seen her for a while.'

"During 1961 and 1962 Our Lady appeared several times each week. The four girls did not always receive the apparition together. Sometimes only one, other times two or three of them saw the vision. It was not always at the same hour of the day. Our Lady appeared many times at night and even early in the morning, in an attitude of sacrifice and penance, at the same hours when Our Lord is most offended by the sins of men.

"The most important message was given on June 18, 1965 on the four year anniversary of the first of the supernatural visitations at Garabandal. Here is what the children were told.

'Many cardinals, many bishops and many priests are on the road to perdition and are taking many souls with them. Less and less importance is being given to the Eucharist. You should turn the wrath of God away from yourselves by your efforts.

'If you ask for His forgiveness with sincere hearts, He will pardon you. I, your mother, through the intercession of Saint Michael the

Archangel, ask you to amend your lives. You are now receiving the last warnings.

'I love you very much and do not want your condemnation. Pray to us with sincerity and we will grant your requests. You should make more sacrifices. Think about the passion of Jesus.'

"In addition, there are three main prophecies that are revealed at Garabandal:

1. *There will be a worldwide event known as THE WARNING whereby God will show every individual how they look through his eyes. To put it another way, each person on earth will see themselves as God sees them. This will be God extending his hand of Mercy to give everyone the chance to reform their lives and return to him before he is forced to extend his hand of Justice when he separates the good from the evil in the return of his Son Jesus in glory.*
2. *Within one year of the warning, God will perform a great miracle at the site of the apparitions in the form of a permanent sign that will remain until the end of time. All of the sick present during the great miracle will be cured.*
3. *There will be a great chastisement (punishment), God as it were extending his hand of Justice to purify the world before the return of Jesus.*

"THE WARNING

1. *Leading up to The Warning, the sun will be seen in the sky as moving and pulsating.*
2. *The Cross of Christ will appear in the sky and visible all around the world:*

    a. *Matthew 24:30* – 'At that time the sign of the Son of Man will appear in the sky, and all the nations of the earth will mourn.'[60]

    b. *Luke 21:25-26* – 'There will be signs in the sun, the moon, and the stars, and on earth nations will be in dismay, perplexed by the roaring of the sea and the waves. People will die of fright in anticipation of what is coming upon the world, for the powers of the heavens will be shaken.'[61]

3. *Two Comets will collide in the sky.*

4. *The sky will turn red.*

5. *Everyone in the world will experience an 'Illumination of Conscience'. This simply means that each one of us will see ourselves as God sees us.*

6. *After The Warning completes, millions around the world will return to the proper worship of God and of living good lives.*

"THE MIRACLE

A miracle will occur in Garabandal within 12 months after the Warning. It will be on a Thursday at 8:30 p.m. on a feast-day of a martyred Saint for the Eucharist. It will happen in the month of April between the 7th and the 17th of the month. It will coincide coincidentally with a very rare but great event within the Church (like the definition of a new dogma). It will be seen by looking up over the area of the Pines and will be visible from the entire surrounding mountainside which will serve as a 'natural' amphitheater. The sick will be cured the unbelievers will be converted. Conchita Gonzalez, the primary visionary, knows the nature of the great miracle as well as the exact date and she will announce the date of the miracle eight days before it happens. It will be able to be filmed, photographed and televised. A Permanent Sign will remain at Garabandal in memory of the miracle as visible proof of our Blessed Mother's love for all humanity. It will be something never before seen upon the earth. It will be indestructible and can be photographed but not touched.

"THE CHASTISEMENT

The Chastisement will be God's hand of justice and will be more terrible than anything we can possibly imagine because it will be the result of the direct intervention of God. It will have nothing to do with wars, revolutions or the hardness of men's hearts. Conchita says, 'If the punishment comes, and I believe it will come, it will come after the promised miracle.'"[62]

"I'm still so amazed at how no one talks about these supernatural apparitions. I mean this one happened only 54 years ago."

"But Jenny, as we've learned, there are those in the hierarchy of the Church that purposely suppress this information from being propagated to the faithful. It's just how it is."

"I guess that's where we come in."

"To me the most amazing thing about these apparitions is the revelation of this event known as The Warning. Can you imagine everyone in the world experiencing God at the same moment in time?"

"So each one of us will see what we look like in God's eyes."

"Right, what we've done right, what we've done wrong and what we need to change. Further on in the journal, Father Mike actually interprets this event to be a miniature judgment where if a person had died at that moment in time and he warranted Heaven, Hell or Purgatory, then he will experience 15 minutes of the place that he would be destined for."

"After reading Sister Lucia's description of Hell, I wouldn't want to have to experience that."

"Well better to experience that now for a short time and change, then to have that place for eternity."

"You got that right, and I guess that's why this event is called God's hand of Mercy. But I'll bet Purgatory is no picnic either."

"Father Mike says in the journal that frequent confession, daily Mass and daily prayer keep us in a 'state of grace' and is perfect preparation for this event because it will guarantee a good experience. I'm thinking that means 15 minutes of Heaven."

"I'll take that."

"Yeah, me too."

"But Chrissy, how about the fact that the sun will be seen in the sky as moving and pulsating before the event even takes place?"

"I wonder if it will be anything like The Miracle of the Sun at Fatima."

"I don't know but whatever it looks like, I just love the fact that we get a sign of its close proximity ahead of time so we can help people prepare."

"It'll be God's way of waking up the world and getting their attention as if to say get ready."

"And then the Cross will appear in the sky. How amazing will that be?"

"And it maps perfectly into the Gospel passages that were written 2000 years ago."

"But look at what it says, people will die of fright."

"Well yeah, two comets are going to collide in the sky. Some people are going to think it's the end of the world and have a heart attack on the spot."

"We have to remember to pray often for those that will die of fright on that day. By the way, does Father Mike mention any other private revelation that confirms this event?"

"Actually he does. There are a couple of others that he points to. He says that it's mentioned four times to the Italian Priest, Father Gobbi, in the blue book.[63] Here I just saw them."

Message #383, May 22, 1988, Heede, Germany (Feast of Pentecost)

(Paragraph d) "The Holy Spirit will come, to establish the glorious reign of Christ, and it will be a reign of grace, of holiness, of love, of justice and of peace. With his divine love, He will open the doors of hearts and illuminate all consciences. Every person will see himself in the burning fire of divine Truth. It will be like a judgment in miniature. And then Jesus Christ will bring his glorious reign in the world."

Message #478, October 2, 1992, Milan, Italy (Feast of the Guardian Angels)

(Paragraph h) "What will come to pass is something so very great that it will exceed anything that has taken place since the beginning of the world. It will be like a judgment in miniature, and each one will see his own life and all he has done in the very light of God."

Message #521, May 22, 1994, Berlin, Germany (Feast of Pentecost)

(Paragraph i) "A new fire will come down from Heaven and will purify all humanity, which has again become pagan. It will be like

a judgment in miniature, and each one will see himself in the light of the very truth of God."

Message #546, June 4, 1995, Vacallo, Switzerland (Feast of Pentecost)

(Paragraph g) "Tongues of fire will come down upon you all, my poor children, so ensnared and seduced by Satan and by all the evil spirits who, during these years, have attained their greatest triumph. And thus, you will be illuminated by this divine light, and you will see your own selves in the mirror of the truth and the holiness of God. It will be like a judgment in miniature, which will open the door of your heart to receive the great gift of divine mercy.

And then the Holy Spirit will work the new miracle of universal transformation in the heart and the life of all: sinners will be converted; the weak will find support; the sick will receive healing; those far away will return to the house of the Father; those separated and divided will attain full unity.

In this way, the miracle of the second Pentecost will take place. It will come with the triumph of my Immaculate Heart in the world."

"That's precisely what the children at Garabandal were told."

"And did you notice, Jenny that 3 out of these 4 messages from the blue book that refer to The Warning were given on the Feast of Pentecost?"

"Well to me that just tells us that The Warning will be by the work of the Holy Spirit."

"Yes, for sure, but it may also be an indication that The Warning itself will take place on the Feast of Pentecost."

"Even if that's true, and it may be, we still don't know the year."

"Understood, but in the journal, Father Mike indicates that The Warning will happen when things in the world are at their worst and we just can't take anymore. When we reach that point, then we'll know our close proximity to The Warning. But he also says this."

"The Feast of Pentecost in addition to being the birthday of the Church when the Holy Spirit descended on the Apostles is also one of the 7 Feasts of the Old Testament. The word comes from the Greek 'pentekoste' (fiftieth) and 'pentekonta' (fifty). Pentecost comes 50 days after Easter beginning with Easter Sunday. In the Old Testament it was known as the Feast of Harvest and also as the Feast of Weeks because it was a week of weeks or 7x7 days after the Feast of Firstfruits. Jesus rose from the dead on the Feast of Firstfruits so this 'natural' feast was fulfilled and transformed by Jesus into the 'supernatural' Feast of the Resurrection celebrated on Easter Sunday. The Holy Spirit descended upon the Apostles on the Old Testament Feast of Harvest and so this 'natural' feast was fulfilled and transformed by The Holy Spirit into the 'supernatural' Feast of Pentecost. So it's important for us to understand that there's an obvious deep connection between these feasts in the Old and New Testaments.

"So Our Blessed Mother mentions The Warning 4 times in her messages to Father Gobbi in the blue book and 3 out of those 4 times it was done on the Feast of Pentecost. She also used the very same words that describe Pentecost to also describe The Warning ('Tongues of fire will come down upon you all'). She then calls it the 'second Pentecost'. So the Warning will clearly be a work of the Holy Spirit and may map to the actual day of Pentecost.

"This would make perfect sense to the Christians because of its connection to the feast of Pentecost but also to the Jews because of its connection to the Feast of Harvest; God as it were gathering his children and bringing them home to him."

"That's impressive."

"I know, right Jenn? Doesn't that make sense?"

"It really does. So what's the date of Pentecost Sunday next year?" Jenny said with a smile.

"I was just thinking the very same thing. I'm already looking it up. Ok, it's May 15, 2016."

"But I believe it's not always a given that the Jewish feast dates coincide with the Christian ones. In order for this theory to resonate, the dates for the feasts must overlap. Chrissy, verify with your phone the feast dates of the Jewish Firstfruits and Weeks/Harvest and compare that to the Christian dates for Easter and Pentecost for 2016, 2017 and 2018."

"Ok, Firstfruits and Weeks for 2016 are April 24 and June 12, and Easter and Pentecost are March 27 and May 15."

"So there is no match for 2016. Now check 2017 and 2018."

"Ok, give me a minute. Firstfruits and Weeks for 2017 are April 16 and June 4, and Easter and Pentecost are April 16 and June 4. Those match. And Firstfruits and Weeks for 2018 are April 1 and May 20, and Easter and Pentecost are also April 1 and May 20. So we have another perfect match."

"So if this theory holds up, then June 4, 2017 and May 20, 2018 would be solid candidates for The Warning. Let's keep those dates in mind. If it's on the mark, we're going to need to get ourselves and others in shape before then. In the end we can't know for sure, but it's nice to have some ideas that we can work from. Are there any other private revelations that Father Mike points to concerning The Warning?"

"Oh yeah, I almost forgot. There is one more. Remember how Father Ramos spoke to us about The Chaplet of Divine Mercy?"

"Yes, we still need to learn that prayer."

"Well that prayer was given to a nun that lived from 1905 to 1938. She received interior locutions like Father Gobbi but she received her locutions from Jesus himself. She was also shown an image of Jesus with white and red rays emanating from his heart."

"Oh, I think I've seen that image. We have one hanging in the back of our Church."

"Right, and have you ever looked to see what it says under the image."

"I don't remember."

"'Jesus, I trust in you.'"

"That's what I heard Jesus say to me, to trust in him." Jenny said as her eyes welled up with tears.

"You ok?"

"Yeah, I'll be alright." She said still drying her tears.

"Well this nun is now a saint. She is Saint Faustina. By the way, the parish that Father Mike was from in Appleton, Wisconsin was Saint Faustina. I just thought I'd throw that in."

"I do remember that."

"So like Father Gobbi she was told to record every word she received from Jesus. She put it all in her diary called, 'Diary of Saint Maria Faustina Kowalska: Divine Mercy in My Soul'. Well in this diary, she recorded these words of Jesus."

"Before I come as the just judge, I am coming first as the King of Mercy. Before the day of justice arrives, there will be given to people

a sign in the heavens of this sort: "All light in the heavens will be extinguished, and there will be great darkness over the whole earth. Then the sign of the cross will be seen in the sky, and from the openings where the hands and the feet of the Savior were nailed will come forth great lights which will light up the earth for a period of time. This will take place shortly before the last day."[64]

"That does sound just like the description of The Warning that you read from the journal. Read that part again."

"Ok, right. Here it is."

"There will be a worldwide event known as THE WARNING whereby God will show every individual how they look through his eyes. To put it another way, each person on earth will see themselves as God sees them. This will be God extending his hand of Mercy to give everyone the chance to reform their lives and return to him before he is forced to extend his hand of Justice when he separates the good from the evil in the return of his Son Jesus in glory."

"Those 2 descriptions about God's hand of Mercy and hand of justice are a good match. And then further on Father Mike also mentions the Cross that will appear in the sky, and that matches as well. So we have three first hand sources that are all describing the same supernatural event."

"Now it's just a matter of when." I said.

"Well what about all the details that the children at Garabandal were given about the great miracle they said would take place within one year after The Warning? It only makes sense that this would give us clues about the date of The Warning as well as the date of the miracle."

"Very true, and there are many hints in there."

"And didn't it say that Conchita knows the exact date of the great miracle?"

"Yes, it did. Here, let's read it over again."

"A miracle will occur in Garabandal within 12 months after the Warning. It will be on a Thursday at 8:30 p.m. on a feast-day of a martyred Saint for the Eucharist. It will happen in the month of April between the 7ᵗʰ and the 17ᵗʰ of the month. It will coincide coincidentally with a very rare but great event within the Church (like the definition of a new dogma). It will be seen by looking up over the area of the Pines and will be visible from the entire surrounding mountainside which will serve as a 'natural' amphitheater. The sick will be cured the unbelievers will be converted. Conchita Gonzalez, the primary visionary, knows the nature of the great miracle as well as the exact date and she will announce the date of the miracle eight days before it happens. It will be able to be filmed, photographed and televised. A Permanent Sign will remain at Garabandal in memory of the miracle as visible proof of our Blessed Mother's love for all humanity. It will be something never before seen upon the earth. It will be indestructible and can be photographed but not touched."

"This can't be that hard to figure out. We know the hundred years are up in October of 2017. Even if it takes a few additional years for Satan to completely lose his power, there are only so many Thursdays in April between the 7ᵗʰ and the 17ᵗʰ that fall between now and then."

"Ok Jenn then let me look at the next four years and list out all Thursdays that fall within those boundaries."

"And we also need to list the Saints whose feast days fall on those days."

"Right, I actually already found a good Catholic website that shows both. Ok, for April 14, 2016 and April 12, 2018, no feast days are celebrated. So those two years are out as potential candidates for the miracle. April 13, 2017 is the feast of Saint Martin I. He was a Pope and Martyr. By the way, this day is also Holy Thursday. And the last one is April 11, 2019. This is the feast of Saint Stanislaus. He was a Bishop and a martyr."

"And a deeper examination into those criteria, specifically, coinciding with 'a feast-day of a martyred Saint for the Eucharist' may reduce that to only one."

"How did you figure that?"

"Right after you mentioned Saint Martin I, I looked him up and did a little reading on him and although he was a Pope and martyr for sure, he does not appear to be a martyr of the Eucharist. He was taken prisoner, beaten and sent into exile in 654 where he eventually died."

"What about Saint Stanislaus?"

"Hold on, I was only just starting to read about him. Ok, he was a Bishop in Poland and was martyred in 1079 by the King of Poland himself who killed Saint Stanislaus get this, while he was in the middle of offering the Holy Sacrifice of the Mass. Now that definitely qualifies Saint Stanislaus as a martyred Saint for the Eucharist."

"So given that information then, this great miracle may not occur until April 11, 2019."

"I don't see how these criteria are satisfied any sooner."

"And how do we solve the coincidental, very rare but great event within the Church that will take place on that same day?"

"There's no way we can know now what that refers to. That will most likely be announced much closer to the event. But I'm sure we are being given this information so that when this rare event is announced, we will recognize it as the final piece to the puzzle. We'll just have to wait and see."

"So that means then, that we can eliminate one of the two dates we identified for The Warning. Remember we said that if Father Mike's theory holds true about Pentecost, then June 4, 2017 and May 20, 2018 would be solid candidates. But given an April 11, 2019 date for the miracle and the fact that The Warning takes place within a year before the miracle, the only date for The Warning that lines up is May 20, 2018."

"Oh, good call Chrissy. That's right. It would make total sense if those dates play out this way."

"It would all fit together nicely just like Father Ramos said it would."

"So let's make sure we engrave those dates in our minds because you know we're going to be asked to backup our claims with logical explanations. We can't act like we haven't thought about it."

"Our approach has been very logical and I suspect that will resonate with most people. But once again, we must make it clear to those that ask that we can't know for sure."

"The one thing, Chrissy, about the apparitions at Garabandal is that unlike Fatima and the locutions given to Father Gobbi, there isn't any mention of the Antichrist. There is mention of the hierarchy leading the faithful away from the one true faith but not of the man of iniquity or of the false prophet."

"It seems to me that both The Warning and the great miracle come late in the game by design after the Antichrist and the false prophet bring their wave of deception."

"Right, that would make The Warning and the miracle God's way of revealing the truth one last time to each individual to expose the falsities and deception accomplished by the 'unholy trinity' of Satan, the Antichrist and the false prophet. It will be God's final act of Mercy to rescue his children before he is forced to allow his hand of justice to fall on the world. Each person will decide for himself whether to accept God or reject him."

"And in so doing God gets the last word and probably rescues billions of people from eternal damnation, bringing them to their senses to return to him before it is too late, and in so doing restores them to their eternal inheritance."

"And once again God will prove his love for his people. It will be amazing to behold."

"Something never before seen." I said.

"But that's what it will take to turn around a world running completely in the wrong direction. By the way, there was one last thing I wanted to ask you about the apparitions at Garabandal."

"What's that?"

"Does Father Mike indicate in the journal anything about whether these apparitions were approved by the Church, like they were at Fatima?"

"Oh, I didn't tell you that part?"

"No."

"He says in the journal that the apparitions at Garabandal have not been officially approved by the Church because no judgment can be made until the events that were predicted there actually take place. So the approval process is in a holding pattern."

"I guess that makes sense. But some of the Fatima prophecies have not taken place yet either."

"Right but he says that in the case of Fatima, the Church had The Miracle of the Sun that was witnessed by 70,000 people. And that miracle validated God's supernatural presence. Garabandal doesn't have anything like that."

"Well not yet anyway. But what Garabandal does have is that some of the information that was revealed there was validated by Saint Faustina, whose work has been approved, and also by the locutions to Father Gobbi in the blue book of the Marian Movement of Priests.

They were given an imprimatur and an official Papal Blessing by Pope John Paul II."

"Right, it can't be summarily dismissed just because its approval status is in a holding pattern."

"Exactly, it has to be taken seriously."

"I'll tell you, the more we study, the more the pieces of this breathtaking end time story come together."

"It is still a daunting task. We have much more to uncover and more to understand."

"I listened again to the directive given by Father Ramos back in Tacoma and there are 2 essential topics we still need to research, the apparitions in La Salette, France and Freemasonry inside and outside of the Church. This should complete the end time's puzzle and equip us with everything we need to help prepare as many as we can for the imminent final confrontation. It's not going to be easy."

"Eternal God, in whom mercy is endless and the treasury of compassion inexhaustible, look kindly upon us and increase Your mercy in us, that in difficult moments we might not despair nor become despondent, but with great confidence submit ourselves to Your holy will, which is Love and Mercy itself. Amen."

CHAPTER 8

LA SALETTE

"Rome will lose the faith and become the seat of the Antichrist."

"What is that?" Jenny asked.

"That's the main prophecy from the apparitions in La Salette, France. We read that line from the journal on that first day when we opened to the page explaining about the Antichrist."

"So this is where he pulled that from, La Salette."

"Right, it's the exact quote."

"Tell me again when that took place?"

"In 1846."

"That was 170 years ago!"

"169 to be exact."

"So just 10 years after our last founding Father died, the world was already receiving precise details about the Antichrist and where he will setup shop?"

"Wait, who was our last founding Father to die?"

"James Madison of course. He died in 1836."

"Only you would know that. Then the answer to your question is yes. But if you think about it, we've already studied passages from the Book of Daniel that tell specifics about the Antichrist, and that's from the Old Testament."

"Good point."

"I still can't believe though that this guy who is the focus of so much attention, written about in numerous places in the Bible and then warned about many times in several private revelations, some dating as far back as 169 years ago, will appear in the world within the next few years."

"I guess we're the lucky ones." Jenny said sarcastically. "But it won't be pretty."

"Amazing though how consistent this one line is with everything we've learned about Fatima and the locutions to Father Gobbi in the blue book."

"That's what makes this stuff so believable is that the information is detailed in different places, in different decades and even different centuries, and yet it warns about the same exact things, the loss of the true faith and the coming of the Antichrist."

"But actually Father Mike points out that the apparitions at La Salette give us remarkable details about the Antichrist that are not recorded in the Bible or in any other private revelation."

"Really, enlighten me."

"Well first let me read you the background from the journal."

"The apparition in La Salette, France took place on September 19, 1846 and was received by two children, 14 year old Melanie Calvat and 11 year old Maximin Giraud. They were taking care of cattle that were grazing high in the hills above La Salette. They saw a bright light that revealed Mary the Mother of Jesus seated on a stone with her hands covering her face. She spoke to them through tears about the need for mankind to repent of its sins and return to God. Some of the messages that the children received were for their time and the decades that followed but some revealed secrets about the end times. I will focus here on the latter."[65]

"Wait Chrissy, before you go any further, let me know this upfront. Were the messages given at La Salette approved by the Church?"

"Yes, it says here they were officially approved by the Church on November 15, 1851."

"And was September 19 the only apparition at La Salette or were there visitations on other days?"

"The apparition on September 19 was the only one that took place in La Salette."

"Ok so now continue."

"I'll read to you the actual words Mary spoke to Melanie concerning the end times as documented in the journal and written down by Melanie herself. Then we can go through what Maximin recorded and from there figure out where La Salette validates what we've already learned and where it's unique."

"Were different secrets given to Melanie and Maximin?"

"Yes. There were times when she spoke so both could hear and other times when only one could hear. Ok, here we go. I'll take it one paragraph at a time."

"The earth will be struck by calamities of all kinds (in addition to plague and famine which will be wide-spread). There will be a series of wars until the last war, which will then be fought by the ten Kings of the Antichrist, all of whom will have one and the same plan and will be the only rulers of the world. Before this comes to pass, there will be a kind of false peace in the world. People will think of nothing but amusement. The wicked will give themselves over to all kinds of sin. But the children of the holy Church, the children of my faith, my true followers, they will grow in their love for God and in all the virtues most precious to me. Blessed are the souls humbly guided by the Holy Spirit! I shall fight at their side until they reach a fullness of years."[66]

"Since 1846, at least involving the United States we had the US-Mexican war, Civil War, World War I, World War II, Korean War, Vietnam War, Gulf War and the Iraq and Afghanistan Wars which continue to this day. But I'm thinking that her reference to the 'last war' probably refers to World War III."

"Right, because that would have to be the big one, the final confrontation." I said.

"I agree. You know I didn't even think of checking but I'm wondering if there are references to a World War III in the blue book. I've been reading that more and more because things are explained in there so well and with great detail. Let me check the online concordance. Hold on. If there are, that would be a good indication that our assertion is correct and this mention of a 'last war' must mean World War III. Ok, there are three references to a third world war in the blue book."[67]

Message #219, January 1, 1981 (Solemnity of Mary, Mother of God)

(Paragraph c) "As has been many times foreseen, a third world-wide war, which will have the terrible capacity of destroying the greater part of the human race, can take place, if men do not seriously resolve to return to God."

Message #441, January 1, 1991, Vicenza, Italy (Solemnity of Mary, Mother of God)

(Paragraph h) "Satan has sung his victory because he has brought sin into souls and division into families, into society, into nations

themselves and between nations. Thus peace has never been so threatened as in your days. You are beginning this new year under the grave threat of a conflict which could become the spark for the outbreak of the terrible third world war."

Message #486, January 1, 1993, Vicenza, Italy (Solemnity of Mary, Mother of God)

(Paragraph t) "At the dawn of this new year, the threat of a terrible third world war is becoming stronger and more worrisome. How many people will have to suffer the scourge of hunger, of famine, of discord, and of fratricidal struggles which will spill much blood on your roads."

"There it is. That's where we're headed. And that second message was given during the Gulf War with Iraq. And it is exactly as she said. That conflict led to the Iraq War in 2003 when the US went in and removed Saddam Hussein. The fight continued all the way up until 2011. Then once we left, it created a vacuum that led directly to the chaos that still exists in that part of the region today. So if the conflict we see expanding in the Middle East eventually leads to World War III, then the Gulf War was indeed the spark."

"And once again, Jenn, we see a pattern. Over 25 years Father Gobbi receives 604 messages of which only 3 refer directly to a third world war, and all three times the messages were given on January 1, the Feast of the Solemnity of Mary, Mother of God."

"Yeah, I noticed that. Though it's hard to know now what that could mean. But as things unfold it may become significant. What about this false peace?"

"Well if you remember correctly, that is also mentioned in the journal entry we read on that first day about the Antichrist. He will bring a false peace to a world at war."

"Yeah, I do remember that. Ok, so let's play this out. The turmoil in the Middle East will most likely escalate between Israel and Iran and they will go to war. The turmoil spreads from the Middle East leading to a Third World War. The Antichrist steps in and offers up a peace agreement that brings an end to all fighting but creates a false peace. He becomes a rock star, people hail him as the messiah, and he takes the lead along with the False Prophet in constructing a new one world economic system and a one world religion that destroys the Church as we know it today. Only a small remnant will remain faithful with many having to suffer martyrdom. And then somewhere in the middle of all this chaos, God steps in to rescue his children as The Warning interrupts time and God's hand of Mercy is extended before his hand of justice is forced to fall with a chastisement that purifies the world for the return of Jesus."

"As crazy as that is, it actually sounds about right. That's what these revelations point to. But there's more. This is where we get details about the Antichrist that are not found anywhere else."

"Nature is asking for vengeance because of man, and she trembles with dread at what must happen to the earth stained with crime. Tremble, earth, and you who proclaim yourselves as serving Jesus Christ and who, on the inside, only adore yourselves, tremble, for God will hand you over to His enemy, because the holy places are in a state of corruption. Many convents are no longer houses of God, but the grazing-grounds of Asmodeas and his like. It will be during this time that the Antichrist will be born of a Hebrew nun, a false virgin who will communicate with the old serpent, the master of

impurity, his father will be B. At birth, he will spew out blasphemy; he will have teeth, in a word; he will be the devil incarnate. He will scream horribly, he will perform wonders; he will feed on nothing but impurity. He will have brothers who, although not devils incarnate like him, will be children of evil. At the age of twelve, they will draw attention upon themselves by the gallant victories they will have won; soon they will each lead armies, aided by the legions of hell.

"The seasons will be altered, the earth will produce nothing but bad fruit, the stars will lose their regular motion, and the moon will only reflect a faint reddish glow. Water and fire will give the earth's globe convulsions and terrible earthquakes which will swallow up mountains, cities, etc...

"Rome will lose the faith and become the seat of the Antichrist.

"The demons of the air together with the Antichrist will perform great wonders on earth and in the atmosphere, and men will become more and more perverted. God will take care of His faithful servants and men of good will. The Gospel will be preached everywhere, and all peoples of all nations will get to know the truth."[68]

"It's all so sobering. And it's hard to believe that the claim is actually going to be made that this guy is the product of a Hebrew virgin birth. Who would fall for that?"

"People who don't know any better will fall for that, and that's most of the world." I said.

"His father will be 'B'? What does that mean?"

"I've read this earlier so I'll just tell you. Maximin gives us the answer with his testimony. 'B' stands for Bishop."

"His father will be a Bishop?"

"I know it's crazy right?"

"Talk about the thing you'd least expect! It's no wonder why she uses the term 'the grazing-grounds of Asmodeas and his like'."

"Yeah, what does that mean?"

"Asmodeas is known as the demon of lust."

"Oh that's rich!"

"But unfortunately it's within the realms of possibility when you're dealing with the forces of evil. But that age of twelve thing; now that's the most intriguing of all. Read that part again."

"At the age of twelve, they will draw attention upon themselves by the gallant victories they will have won; soon they will each lead armies, aided by the legions of hell."

"So he has brothers and it says at the age of twelve 'they'. That would have to mean that he has at least one brother that's the same age. And that would mean he's at least a twin?"

"You know, I didn't pick up on that before but you're right. It also says that they draw attention to themselves because of this. That sounds like the media picks up on it. You would think we would be able to find something about them online. All that stuff is pretty unique."

"I agree. But before any search can be precise, there has to be other criteria that we need to be clear about in order to find a perfect match."

"I don't understand. What do you mean, Jenn?"

"Well look, if he's going to try to convince the world that he's Jesus, then he's going to have to copy every significant thing Jesus did and at the same age that Jesus did them. So as an example, from Sacred Scripture we know that Jesus at the age of twelve was preaching in the Temple. That's unique for a child of that age to be that advanced. So what does the Antichrist do, he leads an army at that same age of twelve. That's also unique for a child of that age to be that advanced. And what else do we know about Jesus? He makes his first public appearance at the age of 30. So when the Antichrist makes his formal entrance onto the world's stage, look for him to be 30."

"So you're saying everything has to fit."

"Right, our search has to find a perfect match. And I think we already have information that fits. We talked about how significant we think it is that the locutions to Father Gobbi stopped just hours or maybe even minutes before the clock turned to 1998. And we know that Father Gobbi was told of the significance of 666+666+666=1998. It marks the time of the Antichrist. I'll bet his accomplishment of leading an army at the age of twelve transpired somewhere around the year 1998. The locutions ended because all the necessary information was given to Father Gobbi according to plan just before the Antichrist makes his first move. And as I pointed out with the turmoil in the Middle East more heightened than it has been in years, his appearance could be imminent."

"And let's also not forget what Father Mike insists in the journal, that the Antichrist will be from the East and not the West."

"I do recall that. And remember as we talked about before, the changing of the Catholic Mass should correspond pretty closely to when the Antichrist makes his first true public appearance so he won't have much more than about 3 years to execute his plans."

"And then that makes our potential dates for The Warning in 2018 and The Miracle in 2019 as reasonable within that time structure."

"Right, and if he's 30 when he first comes on the scene, what age will he be when everything comes to its final conclusion?"

"Oh, 33, the same age that Jesus was when he died on the cross and rose from the dead."

"Exactly, I think this may be the framework that the Antichrist will operate within."

"By the way, here is what Maximin recorded on the topic of the Antichrist."

"In this time the Antichrist will be born of a nun of Hebraic descent, a false virgin, who will have intercourse with the ancient serpent, with the master of impurity and putrefaction. His father will be a bishop. He will perform false miracles and subsist only on vitiating faith. He will have brethren, who will be children of evil but not incarnate devils like himself. Soon they will be at the head of armies, supported by the legions of hell."[69]

"Pretty much the same information but this is where we find out that the "B" referenced by Melanie actually means Bishop." I said.

"That's still so hard to fathom. Did Melanie record anything else?"

"Yes, actually she was told quite a bit more."

"I make an urgent appeal to the earth. I call on the true disciples of the living God who reigns in Heaven; I call on the true followers of Christ made man, the only true Savior of men; I call on my children, the true faithful, those who have given themselves to me so that I may lead them to my divine Son, those whom I carry in my arms, so to speak, those who have lived on my spirit. Finally, I call on the Apostles of the Last Days, the faithful disciples of Jesus Christ who have lived in scorn for the world and for themselves, in poverty and in humility, in scorn and in silence, in prayer and in mortification, in chastity and in union with God, in suffering and unknown to the world. It is time they came out and filled the world with light. Go and reveal yourselves to be my cherished children. I am at your side and within you, provided that your faith is the light which shines upon you in these unhappy days. May your zeal make

you famished for the glory and the honor of Jesus Christ. Fight, children of light, you, the few who can see. For now is the time of all times, the end of all ends.

"The Church will be in eclipse, the world will be in dismay. But now Enoch and Eli will come, filled with the Spirit of God. They will preach with the might of God, and men of good will, will believe in God, and many souls will be comforted. They will make great steps forward through the virtue of the Holy Spirit and will condemn the devilish lapses of the Antichrist. Woe to the inhabitants of the earth! There will be bloody wars and famines, plagues and infectious diseases. It will rain with a fearful hail of animals. There will be thunderstorms which will shake cities, earthquakes which will swallow up countries. Voices will be heard in the air. Men will beat their heads against walls, call for their death, and on another side death will be their torment. Blood will flow on all sides. Who will be the victor if God does not shorten the length of the test? All the blood, the tears and prayers of the righteous, God will relent. Enoch and Eli will be put to death. Pagan Rome will disappear. The fire of Heaven will fall and consume three cities. All the universe will be struck with terror and many will let themselves be lead astray because they have not worshipped the true Christ who lives among them. It is time; the sun is darkening; only faith will survive.

"Now is the time; the abyss is opening. Here is the King of Kings of darkness; here is the Beast with his subjects, calling himself the Savior of the world. He will rise proudly into the air to go to Heaven. He will be smothered by the breath of the Archangel Saint Michael. He will fall, and the earth, which will have been in a continuous series of evolutions for three days, will open up its fiery bowels; and he will have plunged for all eternity with all his followers into the everlasting chasms of hell. And then water and fire

will purge the earth and consume all the works of men's pride and all will be renewed. God will be served and glorified."[70]

"Man, each time we uncover new details of the end times, it is a stark reminder of just how difficult things will become. The world has no idea."

"It's distracted by the temptations of materialism and pleasure while completely unaware of the tsunami of deception and destruction that's heading its way."

"And what about these references to Enoch and Eli?"

"Father Mike indicates that Enoch and Eli translate to the Jews and the Christians. He says that faithful Jews and Christians will take a stand against the Antichrist and the false prophet. But many will be martyred for doing so."

"That's already happening. Christians and Jews are being persecuted around the world right now. And I suspect it's only going to get worse. We can only hope that it doesn't reach our shores. God help us. Then there are these three cities that will be destroyed and by the looks of it one of those cities will be Rome. It's anybody's guess what the other two will be."

"We don't know, but Maximin did record a message that has details that Melanie does not mention."

"If my people continue, what I will say to you will arrive earlier, if it changes a little, it will be a little later.

"France has corrupted the universe, one day it will be punished. The faith will die out in France: three quarters of France will not practice religion anymore, or almost no more, the other part will practice it without really practicing it. Then, after [that], nations will convert, the faith will be rekindled everywhere.

"A great country, now Protestant, in the north of Europe, will be converted; by the support of this country all the other nations of the world will be converted.

"Before all that arrives, great disorders will arrive, in the Church, and everywhere. Then, after [that], our Holy Father the Pope will be persecuted. His successor will be a pontiff that nobody expects. Then, after [that], a great peace will come, but it will not last a long time. A monster will come to disturb it.

"All that I tell you here will arrive in the other century, at the latest in the year two thousand."[71]

"Incredible that in 1846 he is told that depending on the response of the people, these events will be a little earlier or a little later and then names the year two thousand! The faith has died out in France and Pope John Paul I was Pope for only 33 days leading many to believe that behind the scenes his enemies in the Vatican had something to do with his demise. Then his successor Pope John Paul II was a Pope that nobody expected. He is the only Pope from Poland and he was the first non-Italian Pope to be elected in more than 400 years. During his reign things were peaceful but before he arrived there was great turmoil with the Cold War, the Vietnam War and the 1960s in general. The monster must be the Antichrist who arrives on the scene around the year 1998. So it fits."

"The only thing missing" I added, "is the conversion of the great Protestant country in the north of Europe."

"That has to be England, but you're right, it hasn't happened yet. My guess is that the conversion that is spoken about will take place after the truth is revealed with The Warning. That event should wake Nations and bring them back to the proper worship of God."

"That's good to hear because The Warning will definitely be our last chance. You don't want to be on the wrong side of the fence when God's hand of justice falls. There's no coming back from that."

"Very true."

"So that's everything from La Salette. What do you say we search to see if we can find any 12 year olds, from the East, that were twin brothers and who received notoriety for leading armies and winning military victories around the year 1998?" I asked half joking.

"That might be far-fetched for sure but once again remember, anything we find has to be consistent with all the information given to the world at La Salette, the information revealed to Father Gobbi regarding the year 1998, and the first public appearance of the Antichrist at the age of 30 being sometime in the next few years."

"Right, I got it."

And so we searched and incredibly not even 10 minutes later we each found a match.

~

"Are you seeing what I'm seeing?" I asked.

"Twin brothers Johnny and Luther Htoo lead armies at age 12?"

"Yeah, it can't be that easy. I honestly didn't think we'd find anything close. That's crazy."

"They're from Burma. Burma is in the East."

"They were born in 1988. And get this, the people that were inside the house when the twins were born said they heard what sounded like a huge crowd outside the house but when they stepped out to look, there was no one there and there were no footprints."

"They were part of a group of people in Burma called the Karen. In March 1997, at the age of nine, a local pastor brought them to the military leader of the Karen people and told him that God had spoken to the twins and that they would save his people. After the Karen people suffered a brutal defeat by the Burmese army, Luther and Johnny went to the Karen commander and asked for 7 weapons, 7 uniforms and 7 men. In early 1998 they formed their small army and called it "God's Army". Sometime later they lead an attack on the Burmese army with this small fighting group and won! Those that were close to the twins claimed that Johnny and Luther knew the Bible by heart even though they had never studied it and that they would often quote the Old and New Testaments to inspire their troops. Those that fought with them said that it was as if a huge, invisible army was fighting alongside with them. Luther made the claim that he had 250,000 invisible soldiers that he commanded and his brother Johnny had 150,000. They said in battle Luther's eyes would turn red, he would yell commands that sounded like they were coming from an adult commander and he would walk across land mines that wouldn't go off. Soldiers who fought with them claimed to be able to 'brush off bullets like a jungle shower'. Listen to this, in this one incident, Luther sent his men into battle but he stayed in the camp. Those that were with him said while still in the camp, Luther had his rifle pointed at the ground but did not fire a shot. When his men returned from the battle, he asked them how many enemy soldiers had been killed. He was told that twenty were killed. He then showed everyone his rifle and 20 bullets were missing."

"That's crazy stuff. I just found an article that claims that one of them gave three soldiers one 'magic' bullet each and instructed them to use the bullets only when they were in dire need. One of the three soldiers didn't believe the bullet had any magical powers and shot the bullet at a tree. When he subsequently examined the tree he found ten bullet holes. It also talks about how the twins claimed to be devout Baptist Christians and how they claimed to have never cried. The

Karen villagers believed that the twins had supernatural powers. And others said that they had uncanny skills for settling disputes."[72] [73] [74]

"As crazy as it sounds there is so much here that is a perfect match to what Melanie and Maximin were told in 1846. Chrissy, read again what they were told about being assisted by legions from Hell."

"Here's the quote from Melanie's writings."

"At the age of twelve, they will draw attention upon themselves by the gallant victories they will have won; soon they will each lead armies, aided by the legions of hell."

"And here's the one from Maximin."

"Soon they will be at the head of armies, supported by the legions of hell."

"These details are identical to what Luther claimed and to what those that fought alongside testified."

"But not just in battle, how about the possibility that those legions were present outside the house at the time of their birth." I said.

"It's also significant that they start with 7 men, 7 uniforms and 7 weapons. Seven is used all throughout the Bible and represents perfection."

"And of course they call their army, 'God's Army' and they initiated their efforts to form their army in early 1998. Another match to what Father Gobbi was told and what we observed with Father Gobbi's last message."

"At the age of twelve in the year 2000 they were probably at the height of their influence and that's when the media picked up on it."

"This is a remarkable match. Let's be honest, did either of us really think we would find anything like this? I know I didn't."

"No way, and let's not forget the uncanny skills at settling disputes. That's significant. Remember that the Antichrist will propose a Mideast peace plan that will work, will bring a false peace and this success will be what elevates his popularity around the world."

"If one of these two is truly the Antichrist, then which one is he?" I asked.

"From what we've just read, Luther is clearly more the leader and if he is the future Antichrist, his name sure is fitting, wouldn't you say?"

"What do you mean?"

"Hello, Lucifer."

"Oh right, I kind of missed the obvious there. But can it really be this easy? "

"Yeah, it is if you know what you're looking for. Most people wouldn't have a clue about an apparition in La Salette, but it's all there. You just have to know where to look and thanks to Father Mike, we do."

"Ok, get this. Just for kicks, I looked up what the name Luther means. You're not going to believe this."

"What does it mean?"

"It means, 'Famous in war'."

"If the glove fits, you must admit."

"Nice!" I said laughing. "I also found an article written in 2013 that updates the whereabouts of Luther and Johnny. Luther now lives in Sweden where he studied economics and history and where he married a Karen woman. They had a child together but they have since divorced. Johnny is in a refugee camp back home. Here's a picture of the two of them taken two years ago."

"Luther certainly doesn't look the part, does he?"

"No, not at all."

"Wait, you just said he's in Sweden now. I read a BBC article just yesterday about a hi-tech office block in Sweden that's implanting

RFID chips in the hands of the company employees that are part of the block. They use the chips to access the building, use the copier and even pay for their lunches. We now know that RFID chips will be implemented worldwide and will fulfill the Book of Revelation prophecy for the mark of the beast.[75] Is it possible that there's a connection here and he is somehow involved behind the scenes with this trial? I know some might say that is circumstantial but even if you discount it, with regard to the other items, man he is a perfect match! I'll tell you what, if he's not the one, then he has the unfortunate and unique distinction of sharing precise, prophesied milestones and characteristics with the Antichrist. I mean just look at all this.

- He's from the East.
- He has a twin brother to satisfy, 'at the age of twelve, they'.
- Witnesses claimed great crowds were present at their birth but no one was visible.
- Both he and his brother drew attention to themselves by leading armies to gallant victories at the age of twelve.
- He and his brother formed their army in 1998. (666+666+666)
- They asked for 7 men, 7 uniforms and 7 weapons. (The number 7 has deep significance in the Bible as it is the number for perfection and completeness.)
- They called their army, 'God's Army'.
- They claimed to be devout Christians and to know the Bible by heart, quoting the Old and New Testaments to inspire their troops.
- Fellow soldiers claimed invisible legions fought by their side and that they were able to 'brush off bullets like a jungle shower'.[76]
- They walked fearlessly across land mines that never went off.
- They shouted commands in battle like generals.

- Luther's eyes would turn red in the heat of the battle.
- People that knew them claimed they possessed supernatural powers.
- Luther himself claimed that he commanded an invisible army of 250,000 and his brother commanded an invisible army of 150,000. ('aided by the legions of hell')
- They were known to have uncanny abilities to settle disputes. (He will negotiate a false peace.)
- He moved to Sweden where he cleaned up his act and studied economics. It's also in Sweden where they are trialing the use of an RFID chip to allow employees to access the building they work in, use the copier and even pay for lunch. (The Antichrist will orchestrate a new one world economic system and implement a new one world currency that will utilize the mark of the beast, a RFID chip that will be implanted under the skin of individuals to allow them to buy and sell.)

"I got it and that's all good, but there is still one glaring requirement that must also be satisfied." I said.

"What's that?"

"If Luther is the Antichrist, then according to the journal, not just the triple sum of '666' must play a role in his life, namely the year 1998, but also his name must add in Hebrew to '666'."

"Where does that come from?"

"He says that it's right from the book of Revelation.

Revelation 13:18
'Wisdom is needed here; one who understands can calculate the number of the beast, for it is a number that stands for a person. His number is six hundred and sixty-six.'

"The same passage we use to triple sum '666' also requires that the Hebrew sum of the actual name of the Antichrist result in '666'. Apparently that passage has a double meaning."

"Right, that's the whole Emperor Nero thing. Well how do we figure that out?"

"Father Mike explains that you translate his name into Hebrew. Then you populate his Hebrew name into a Hebrew Gematria Calculator and see what number results."

"I never heard of a Hebrew Gematria Calculator but let me quickly look online. Is there anything we can't find online these days? And of course there is one. Crazy! So let me translate 'Luther' from English to Hebrew. Ok, I get this 'רתול', whatever that is. I insert it into the calculator in the field labeled 'LETTER' and then select 'ACTIVATE SOFIT' and it calculates to '636'. That's close but it's not '666'."

"Yeah but you have to use both his first and last names. Translate 'Luther Htoo' and insert that result."

"Ok, 'Luther Htoo' translates to 'הטה רתול' in Hebrew and calculates to '655'. Closer still but it's not '666'."

"There must be a trick to this."

We both thought for a while and then Jenny came up with this.

"How about we try this? In the 17 minute documentary we watched on Johnny and Luther done by the ABC affiliate out of Australia, they pronounced the twins' last name as 'Too' or 'To' with the 'H' completely silent."

"It's worth a shot. Try 'Luther Too'."

"'Luther Too' translates to 'ידמ רתול' in Hebrew and calculates to '690'. It's still not '666'."

"Only one option left."

"Ok, last try, 'Luther To' translates to 'ל רתול' and calculates to, shut up!"

"What?"

"That's it!! Look, it calculates to '666'."

"No way! That's crazy!"

"It is him!"

"This is so unbelievable. You know not even Father Mike figured this out."

"Chalk one up for us."

"I'm numb. I guess I never really expected this to actually work out."

"Me neither. That seals the deal. But that means he doesn't turn 30 until 2018. That's a bit later than we thought but I still firmly believe that the Antichrist will appear on the world's stage at the age of 30 because that's when Jesus began his public ministry. He's going to try to copy everything Jesus did in order to completely deceive the world."

"Maybe it will take that long for the Mideast to spiral out of control." I said.

"That's quite possible. But here's the thing, if the Antichrist is from the East and draws attention to himself and his twin brother by leading armies to gallant victories at the age of 12 aided by the legions of hell in or around the year 1998, then we should be able to find evidence of it. And we did, we found Luther. But we also found no one else. So if the Antichrist is not Luther, then where is the match that's even remotely close to this one?"

"There isn't one."

"Eternal God, in whom mercy is endless and the treasury of compassion inexhaustible, look kindly upon us and increase Your mercy in us, that in difficult moments we might not despair nor become despondent, but with great confidence submit ourselves to Your holy will, which is Love and Mercy itself. Amen."

CHAPTER 9

FREEMASONRY

Up early as usual, sitting in my favorite surfside recliner beach chair, looking out over the ocean from the high perch of our backyard lawn, I couldn't help but capture the breathtaking morning sunrise. The radiant color transformation from red to orange exploded off the horizon as a bright white light lit up the sky. The glistening colors melted perfectly together, reflecting off the water as if to tease the ocean to celebrate its rise. Slowly the twilight sky surrendered to the brilliant rays of the sun as it began to warm the morning air. As I marveled at this site, I couldn't help but wonder how anyone could witness this crescendo of beauty and not believe that there is a God.

Watching the lobster boats head out to sea, I pondered how life will change in this beautiful place we call home. The coming years were sure to bring untold sorrows. The details that Jenny and I were uncovering promised to change life as we knew it to be. Only prayer can mitigate what is coming. If only we could convince the world of that.

As I drifted off in my thoughts, the calm was suddenly interrupted as a chair was placed next to mine. I was surprised to see Jenny up early with blue book in hand.

"What are you doing up so early?" I asked still curious as to what would wake her at the crack of dawn.

"I was bothered by the fact that we never did discuss all those references to Freemasonry in the blue book locutions to Father Gobbi regarding the Fatima secrets. I've been reading this book more and more and the warnings about Freemasonry are everywhere."[77]

"That was one of the topics that Father Ramos told us was critical to understand."

"I mean just listen to this."

Message #406, June 13, 1989, Como, Italy (Anniversary of the Second Apparition at Fatima)

(Paragraph g) "The black beast like a leopard indicates Freemasonry; the beast with the two horns like a lamb indicates Freemasonry infiltrated into the interior of the Church, that is to say, ecclesiastical Masonry, which has spread especially among the members of the hierarchy. This Masonic infiltration, in the interior of the Church, was already foretold to you by me at Fatima, when I announced to you that Satan would enter in even to the summit of the Church. If the task of Masonry is to lead souls to perdition, bringing them to the worship of false divinities, the task of ecclesiastical Masonry on the other hand is that of destroying Christ and his Church, building a new idol, namely a false christ and a false church."

(Paragraph l) "Thus errors are spread in every part of the Catholic Church itself. Because of the spread of these errors, many are moving away today from the true faith, bringing to fulfillment the prophecy which was given to you by me at Fatima: 'The times

will come when many will lose the true faith.' The loss of faith is apostasy. Ecclesiastical Masonry works, in a subtle and diabolical way, to lead all into apostasy."

"So Freemasonry poses two different threats, one inside the Church and the other outside the Church?"

"Yes and in both cases it is formidable." Jenny explained. "Those references to the Black Beast and the Beast like a Lamb are right out of the book of Revelation. This is serious stuff."

"Well what is it about Freemasonry that makes it so dangerous?"

"I looked into that and one of its main charters is the outright destruction of the Catholic Church. But I also looked into its history and found some interesting facts that explain where they're coming from. By 1717 the old Masonic lodges were almost non-existent. They were resurrected in England in 1722 with the establishment of the Grand Lodge of England where they introduced a new 'Book of Constitutions'. This signaled a break from the old order and created a completely new direction. In July of 1889, the Grand Orient of France organized an international Masonic congress to bring about a universal Freemasonry and promote the Masonic ideals. Their goal was the establishment of a 'universal social republic'.[78] Can anybody say 'New World Order'? They also insisted that the primary education of children must be accomplished by the schools with little or no influence from the Church or even their own parents.[79] That sounds just like the public schools of today. And in their own words:

'Masonry, which prepared the Revolution of 1789, has the duty to continue its work.'[80]

"That last line is significant. It's a reference to the French Revolution which turned French society completely upside down through violent rebellion against the French Monarchy and the Catholic Church in France. France remained in turmoil for decades after that revolution. And yet this is precisely what Freemasonry sought to export to the world coming out of that congress in 1889."

"But the Church must have been aware of what the forces of Freemasonry were up to." I said.

"Actually they were. I've been reading all about the history of this. Documents were leaked to them over the years and as early as 1738 the Church began issuing papal pronouncements and encyclicals warning about the dangers of Freemasonry. This continued for 220 years all the way through the pontificate of Pius XII which ended in 1958. But probably the most telling detail about Freemasonry is their issuance in the 1820s of a secret document put out by the highest lodge of the Carbonari. The document was known as the 'Permanent instruction of the Alta Vendita' and it disclosed the long term marching orders for European Freemasonry. It presented an insidious strategy to effectively neutralize the Catholic Church by infiltrating it with the liberal and progressive principles of the French Revolution so that eventually they would be adopted into its doctrines and practices. These included notions of Humanism, the idea that man is of primary importance and not God, religious pluralism, the idea that an individual must accept religious beliefs different from his own as valid, as well as the insistence that all religions are equal. Their thinking was that if this plan was successful, it would one day lead to the election of a liberal Pope that would tolerate their views and even act to incorporate them into the Church's teachings. If successful, this would advance their cause and eliminate the Church as their staunchest critic. The document was leaked to Pope Gregory XVI somewhere around the 1840s and in 1861 Pope Pius IX had it published in order to expose the plans of Freemasonry to destabilize the Church from within. On April 20, 1884, Pope Leo XIII issued his encyclical on Freemasonry, 'Humanum Genus', where he requested that Catholic leaders 'tear off the mask from Freemasonry and make plain to all what it really is.'[81] So for a very long time the Church was able to expose their plans and prevent them from coming to fruition in any way."

"But what The Blessed Mother revealed to Father Gobbi most recently in the blue book is that Freemasonry has successfully implemented their plan to infiltrate the Catholic Church."

"Yes, that's right. And we've seen that from what we've already discovered with the efforts from within the Church to suppress the Prayer to Saint Michael, the consecration of Russia and the third secret of Fatima as well as the silencing of Sister Lucia."

"Father Mike points out in the journal much of what you just said that there have been efforts within the Church to minimize the supernatural and focus primarily on the needs of man. He calls it the over-emphasis on social justice."

"Right and you can see how that paves the way for a one world religion. The supernatural as you say is de-emphasized leaving only an emphasis on the natural. This means that concepts like sin, eternal salvation, sanctifying grace and the Sacraments go out the window. The Holy Sacrifice of the Mass is changed to simply a remembrance of the last supper and no longer a re-presenting to God the Father of the actual once-for-all perfect Sacrifice of Jesus, true God and true man, made on the cross at Calvary for the purpose of accomplishing perfect reparation for sin. Human existence is reduced to purely flesh and blood material interests. In this way all religions can unite on issues involving feeding the poor, eliminating poverty, improving the environment and worldwide economic growth. God is completely removed from the picture and you arrive at the ultimate goal of Freemasonry, humanism accompanied by practical atheism, a claim to believe in God but act as though he doesn't exist."

"Wow, that's depressing."

"But this is precisely what Mary the Mother of Jesus is trying to point out in these locutions to Father Gobbi. Her point is that her son died to save our eternal souls, not to solve the world's material problems. Just listen again to what she has to say and how she says it."

Message #406, June 13, 1989, Como, Italy (Anniversary of the Second Apparition at Fatima)

(Paragraphs h through n) 'Jesus Christ is the Son of the living God, He is the Word Incarnate, He is true God and true Man because He unites in his divine Person human nature and divine nature. Jesus, in the Gospel, has given his most complete definition of Himself, saying that He is the Truth, the Way and the Life.

'Jesus is the Truth, because He reveals the Father to us, speaks his definitive word to us, and brings all divine revelation to its perfect fulfillment.

'Jesus is the Life, because He gives us divine life itself, with the grace merited by Him through redemption, and He institutes the sacraments as efficacious means which communicate grace.

Jesus is the Way which leads to the Father, by means of the Gospel which He has given us, as the way to follow to attain salvation.

'Jesus is the Truth because it is He -- the living Word -- who is the font and seal of all divine revelation. And so ecclesiastical Masonry works to obscure his divine word, by means of natural and rational interpretations and, in the attempt to make it more understandable and acceptable, empties it of all its supernatural content. Thus errors are spread in every part of the Catholic Church itself. Because of the spread of these errors, many are moving away today from the true faith, bringing to fulfillment the prophecy

which was given to you by me at Fatima: 'The times will come when many will lose the true faith.' The loss of the faith is apostasy. Ecclesiastical Masonry works, in a subtle and diabolical way, to lead all into apostasy.

'Jesus is the Life because He gives grace. The aim of ecclesiastical Masonry is that of justifying sin, of presenting it no longer as an evil but as something good and of value. Thus one is advised to do this as a way of satisfying the exigencies of one's own nature, destroying the root from which repentance could be born, and is told that it is no longer necessary to confess it. The pernicious fruit of this accursed cancer, which has spread throughout the whole Church, is the disappearance everywhere of individual confession. Souls are led to live in sin, rejecting the gift of life which Jesus has offered us.

'Jesus is the Way which leads to the Father, by means of the Gospel. Ecclesiastical Masonry favors those forms of exegesis which give it a rationalistic and natural interpretation, by means of the application of the various literary genres, in such a way that it becomes torn to pieces in all its parts. In the end, one arrives at denying the historical reality of miracles and of the resurrection and places in doubt the very divinity of Jesus and his salvific mission.'

"It's exactly like you said, Jenny. She clearly indicates that Freemasonry destroys the supernatural leaving only the pursuit of purely natural, human interests."

"And the reason why this strategy is so attractive is that it sounds and feels good. It's a call to love your neighbor which on the surface sounds good. But it's brilliantly deceptive because it eliminates God from the process, so anyone that goes along, falls into apostasy by indirectly denying the work of salvation and puts their soul on a path that could lead to perdition. Of course this is Satan's ultimate goal, the destruction of the soul. So the False Prophet and the Antichrist will pick up the torch to a framework that Freemasonry spent centuries providing both inside and outside the Church. And then they'll work together to lure people down this road of denial of God and denial of their birthright to an eternal inheritance in Heaven."

"Boy that is clever."

"Yup, planned and orchestrated from the depths of Hell."

"So you said that Freemasonry works both inside and outside the Church? This clearly explains their efforts inside the Church but what about outside, in the world as a whole? How does it operate out there?"

"That's also clearly explained."

Message #405, June 3, 1989, Milan, Italy (Feast of the Immaculate Heart of Mary)

(Paragraphs c, d, e) *"In this terrible struggle, there comes up from the sea, to the aid of the Dragon, a beast like a leopard.*

"If the Red Dragon is Marxist atheism, the Black Beast is Freemasonry. The Dragon manifests himself in the force of his power; the Black Beast, on the other hand, acts in the shadow, keeps out of sight and hides himself in such a way as to enter in everywhere. He has the claws of a bear and the mouth of a lion, because he works everywhere with cunning and with the means of social communication, that is to say, through propaganda. The seven heads indicate the various Masonic lodges, which act everywhere in a subtle and dangerous way.

"This Black Beast has ten horns and, on the horns, ten crowns, which are signs of dominion and royalty. Masonry rules and

governs throughout the whole world by means of the ten horns. The horn, in the biblical world, has always been an instrument of amplification, a way of making one's voice better heard, a strong means of communication.

(Paragraph i) "If the Lord has communicated his Law with the Ten Commandments, Freemasonry spreads everywhere, through the power of its ten horns, a law which is completely opposed to that of God.

(Paragraph s, t, u) "In this way souls become driven along the perverse and wicked road of disobedience to the laws of the Lord, become submerged in sin and are thus prevented from receiving the gift of grace and of the life of God.

"To the seven theological and cardinal virtues, which are the fruit of living in the grace of God, Freemasonry counters with the diffusion of the seven capitol vices, which are the fruit of living habitually in the state of sin. To faith it opposes pride; to hope, lust; to charity, avarice; to prudence, anger; to fortitude, sloth; to justice, envy; to temperance, gluttony.

"Whoever becomes a victim of the seven capitol vices is gradually led to take away the worship that is due to God alone, in order to give it to false divinities, who are the very personification of all these vices. And in this consists the greatest and most horrible blasphemy. This is why on every head of the Beast there is written a blasphemous name. Each Masonic lodge has the task of making a different divinity adored.

(Paragraph C) "The task of the Masonic lodges is that of working today, with great astuteness, to bring humanity everywhere to disdain the holy Law of God, to work in open opposition to the Ten Commandments, and to take away the worship due to God alone in order to offer it to certain false idols which become extolled and adored by an ever increasing number of people: reason, flesh, money, discord,

domination, violence, pleasure. Thus souls are precipitated into the dark slavery of evil, of vice and of sin and, at the moment of death and of the judgment of God, into the pool of eternal fire which is hell."

"To put this all in perspective and to better understand these references, here are the passages from the Book of Revelation chapter 13 that correlate to Freemasonry; first as the 'Beast like a Leopard' operating in the world outside the Church." Jenny explained.

Revelation 13: 1-10
"Then I saw a beast come out of the sea with ten horns and seven heads; on its horns were ten diadems, and on its heads blasphemous name[s]. The beast I saw was like a leopard, but it had feet like a bear's, and its mouth was like the mouth of a lion. To it the dragon gave its own power and throne, along with great authority. I saw that one of its heads seemed to have been mortally wounded, but this mortal wound was healed. Fascinated, the whole world followed after the beast. They worshiped the dragon because it gave its authority to the beast; they also worshiped the beast and said, 'Who can compare with the beast or who can fight against it?' The beast was given a mouth uttering proud boasts and blasphemies, and it was given authority to act for forty-two months. It opened its mouth to utter blasphemies against God, blaspheming his name and his dwelling and those who dwell in heaven. It was also allowed to wage war against the holy ones and conquer them, and it was granted authority over every tribe, people, tongue, and nation. All the inhabitants of the earth will worship it, all whose names were not written from the foundation of the world in the book of life, which belongs to the Lamb who was slain. Whoever has ears ought to hear these words. Anyone destined for captivity goes into

captivity. Anyone destined to be slain by the sword shall be slain by the sword. Such is the faithful endurance of the holy ones."

"And here are the passages from the Book of Revelation chapter 13 that correlate to Freemasonry as the 'Beast like a Lamb' operating from inside the Church." Jenny continued.

Revelation 13: 11-18
"Then I saw another beast come up out of the earth; it had two horns like a lamb's but spoke like a dragon. It wielded all the authority of the first beast in its sight and made the earth and its inhabitants worship the first beast, whose mortal wound had been healed. It performed great signs, even making fire come down from heaven to earth in the sight of everyone. It deceived the inhabitants of the earth with the signs it was allowed to perform in the sight of the first beast, telling them to make an image for the beast who had been wounded by the sword and revived. It was then permitted to breathe life into the beast's image, so that the beast's image could speak and [could] have anyone who did not worship it put to death. It forced all the people, small and great, rich and poor, free and slave, to be given a stamped image on their right hands or their foreheads, so that no one could buy or sell except one who had the stamped image of the beast's name or the number that stood for its name. Wisdom is needed here; one who understands can calculate the number of the beast, for it is a number that stands for a person. His number is six hundred and sixty-six."

"And this is how we know that the 'Beast like a Lamb' is properly interpreted as a force operating from within the Church."

Message #406, June 13, 1989, Milan, Italy (Feast of the Immaculate Heart of Mary)

(Paragraphs e, f) "The lamb, in Holy Scripture, has always been a symbol of sacrifice. On the night of the exodus, the lamb is sacrificed, and, with its blood, the doorposts of the houses of the Hebrews are sprinkled, in order to remove them from the punishment which on the contrary strikes all the Egyptians. The Hebrew Pasch recalls this fact each year, through the immolation of a lamb, which is sacrificed and consumed. On Calvary, Jesus Christ sacrifices Himself for the redemption of humanity; He Himself becomes our Pasch and becomes the true Lamb of God who takes away all the sins of the world.

"The beast has on its head two horns like those of a lamb. To the symbol of the sacrifice, there is intimately connected that of the priesthood: the two horns. The high priest of the Old Testament wore a headpiece with two horns. The bishops of the Church wear a mitre with two horns to indicate the fullness of their priesthood."

"Incredible! So then all of chapter 13 in the Book of Revelation refers to Freemasonry." I said.

"Yes, in its two forms, first as the 'Beast like a Leopard' operating in the world and second as the 'Beast like a Lamb' operating from within the Church. But it even goes deeper than that. I also took the liberty of looking into the journal to see if Father Mike had the same take on Freemasonry. I found that he did but he took it even deeper. He indicated that just as Freemasonry gives rise to two beasts that operate in the world and then from within the Church, each of these two manifestations of Freemasonry then give rise to an individual. He says that this part of the passage from Revelation that we read previously about the 'Beast like a Leopard' indicates the Antichrist."

> *"The beast was given a mouth uttering proud boasts and blasphemies, and it was given authority to act for forty-two months. It opened its mouth to utter blasphemies against God, blaspheming his name and his dwelling and those who dwell in heaven. It was also allowed to wage war against the holy ones and conquer them, and it was granted authority over every tribe, people, tongue, and nation. All the inhabitants of the earth will worship it, all whose names were not written from the foundation of the world in the book of life, which belongs to the Lamb who was slain."*

"Then he says that this part about the 'Beast like a Lamb' indicates that an individual from within the Church will perform these great signs, namely the False Prophet."

> *"It performed great signs, even making fire come down from heaven to earth in the sight of everyone. It deceived the inhabitants of the earth with the signs it was allowed to perform in the sight of the first beast, telling them to make an image for the beast who had been wounded by the sword and revived."*

"So let me get this straight. Freemasonry gives rise to the 'Beast like a Leopard' operating in the world which then gives rise to the Antichrist? And then separately but simultaneously, Freemasonry gives rise to the 'Beast like a Lamb' operating from within the Church which then gives rise to the False Prophet?" I asked.

"Right, the False Prophet is the precursor to the Antichrist, he sets the stage and points to the Antichrist as the messiah when he appears, just as John the Baptist was the precursor to Jesus and pointed to Jesus as the actual Messiah when he appeared. Then the False Prophet and the Antichrist will work together to try to deceive both the faithful and the rest of the world. As to who from the within the Catholic Church is the False Prophet, Father Mike posits that it will be a Cardinal that will rise to great power. He points to these lines in the Book of Daniel as proof."

Daniel 9: 26-27
"After the sixty-two weeks an anointed one shall be cut down with no one to help him. And the people of a leader who will come shall destroy the city and the sanctuary. His end shall come in a flood; until the end of the war, which is decreed, there will be desolation. For one week he shall make a firm covenant with the many; Half the week he shall abolish sacrifice and offering; In their place shall be the desolating abomination until the ruin that is decreed is poured out upon the desolator."

"He says to take notice that 'an anointed one' is pushed aside to make room for the False Prophet and that the Hebrew word that is used by Daniel for 'leader' is actually 'nagiyd' which translates to 'prince'. Cardinals in the Catholic Church are called princes of the Church. He also says that the reference to 'one week' means a period of seven years, one year for each day of the week. Understanding that then it appears that the False Prophet will rule for about 7 years and 'half the week' interprets to 3 ½ years which is exactly what we have already learned is the period of time that the Holy Sacrifice of the Mass will be abolished, called the 'desolating abomination'. Notice also that the 3 ½ years is the same period of time as the 42 month reference we just read."

"Once again, it all fits together." I said.

"Just like Father Ramos said it would. But there is one more piece of information that really seals the deal. Check this out. As proof that it really is Freemasonry that gives rise to the Antichrist. Let's look again at the last line from Revelation 13."

"Wisdom is needed here; one who understands can calculate the number of the beast, for it is a number that stands for a person. His number is six hundred and sixty-six."

"We already talked about this passage and the two ways to interpret this number as given to us in the journal. But I found in the blue book where Father Mike acquired the notion of adding 666 three times to arrive at the year 1998. It has to do with the Antichrist for sure, but it's Freemasonry that provides the platform for the Antichrist to step onto and make his impressive debut as a man of peace."

Message #407, June 17, 1989, Milan, Italy

(Paragraph p) "666 indicated thrice, that is to say, for the third time, expresses the year 1998, nineteen hundred and ninety-eight. In this period of history, Freemasonry, assisted by its ecclesiastical form, will succeed in its great design; that of setting up an idol to put in the place of Christ and of His Church; A false Christ and a false Church. Consequently, the statue built in honor of the first beast, to be adored by all the inhabitants of the earth and which will seal with its mark all those who want to buy or sell, is that of the Antichrist. You have thus arrived at the peak of the purification, of the great tribulation and of the apostasy. The apostasy will be, as of then, generalized because almost all will

follow the false Christ and false Church. Then the door will be open for the appearance of the man or of the very person of the Antichrist!"

"So you see Freemasonry is the foundation that gives rise to the Antichrist. Its diabolical methods are all about deceiving the world to accept a false Christ and a false Church and reject the true Christ and his true Church."

"This is deception at its finest." I insisted.

"It is. But there is also another approved private revelation that I found of which very few people are aware and that we can't overlook. And it totally backs up all this stuff about Freemasonry."

"What's that?"

"Beginning on February 2, 1594 and ending on December 8, 1634, in Quito, Ecuador, Venerable Mother Mariana of Jesus Torres received many visitations from Our Blessed Mother under the title of Our Lady of Good Success. Many of the messages that she received were prophecies about the twentieth century and about Freemasonry."

"No way, what was she told?"

"Here, listen to this. I found three quotes that reference Freemasonry as a force for evil in our day."

"Thus I make it known to you that from the end of the 19th century and shortly after the middle of the 20th century ... the passions will erupt and there will be a total corruption of customs (morals), for Satan will reign almost completely by means of the Masonic sects."

"During that epoch the Church will find herself attacked by terrible hordes of the Masonic sect, and this ... will be agonizing because of the corruption of customs, unbridled luxury, the impious press, and

secular education. The vices of impurity, blasphemy, and sacrilege will dominate in this time of depraved desolation, and that one who should speak out will be silent..."

"... the Masonic sects, having infiltrated all the social classes, would subtly introduce its teaching into domestic ambiences in order to corrupt the children, and the Devil would glory in dining upon the exquisite delicacy of the hearts of children."[82]

"But, Chrissy, what's amazing about this, is that as we've already learned, Freemasonry didn't begin to develop into the kind of force it is today until the early 1700s. So this information was given 100 years before Freemasonry was even a cause for concern. And in these messages, Freemasonry is once again identified as both a danger for the Church and the world, exactly as we were discussing."

"Our Lady of Good Success, pray for us! So even after all these warnings from Heaven, the world will be none the wiser. We can't let them get away with this. We have to expose Freemasonry as the clear and present danger that it is."

"Then there's only one way we can possibly succeed in making a difference."

"How is that?"

"We're going to have to pray fervently for God to grant us His Wisdom, His Strength, His Perseverance, and His Courage. Without him, we are nothing and without his help, we fail miserably. And then we're going to have to act according to his Holy Will, holding back nothing to expose this secret sect and their diabolical activity both within the Church and the world."

"Eternal God, in whom mercy is endless and the treasury of compassion inexhaustible, look kindly upon us and increase Your mercy in us, that in difficult moments we might not despair nor become despondent, but with great confidence submit ourselves to Your holy will, which is Love and Mercy itself. Amen."

CHAPTER 10

SHEEP IN THE MIDST OF WOLVES

O ur study of Freemasonry completed our research into the topics covered by Father Mike in the Journal and recommended by
Father Ramos. Even though only three months had passed since we first
began this journey back in Tacoma, we felt as though we had absorbed
the essentials of Father Mike's research. Both Jenny and I were still
overwhelmed by the task we had been given, but we were both committed to persevere in our efforts to warn the world about the dangerous
deception that is about to unfold.

Guided by God's grace we devised a strategy to spread the truth
about the end times. We developed three separate pamphlets that
summarized all we had learned about the Prayer to Saint Michael,
the visions of Pope Leo XIII and Pius X, the Miracle of the Sun,
the messages of Fatima, Garabandal and La Salette. We exposed
Freemasonry for the danger that it is and warned of the imminent
World War. We alerted of the changing of the Mass and finally the
appearance of the Antichrist. Our plan was to first distribute them
within our local parish and then gradually branch out to other parishes around the diocese. But you know what they say about the best
laid plans.

Friday, September 11, 2015 saw the biggest drop in stock market history. Sharply rising interest rates and the collapse of world markets created a domino effect that caused investors to lose confidence in the market and pull back. Within 24 hours the Dow Jones Industrial Average had lost over 3000 points. Panic ensued as the dollar was being dumped worldwide as the official reserve currency. The price of Gold soared from $1200 an ounce to $4200 in three days and then over the next three weeks it skyrocketed to $9000. Over the next month the Dow fell an additional 7000 points. When the dust had settled the stock market had lost over 50% of its value. During subsequent weeks businesses were forced to cutback which led to massive layoffs. Churches were overflowing as people everywhere turned to God for help. And it was with this as a backdrop that we set out to spread the truth about the times we are living through.

People hungered for an explanation for what was happening and the pamphlets offered them the truth and pointed the way out of the chaos. As word spread, we were inundated with requests for copies not just from within our diocese but from diocese all over the country. Donations poured in from all over to our online funding page. Within the first three months we distributed over 144,000 pamphlets. Our efforts turned into full time jobs as we were forced to hire a staff of seven to help with logistics and keep up with demand. Translations were done for Spanish as the distribution numbers continued to increase.

But not all reaction was positive. We received letters from six Bishops around the country demanding that we cease and desist from all distribution of our pamphlets within their diocese. They claimed that it infringed on their authority to propagate the faith and their responsibility to protect the faithful from any dangerous outside influence. But we were not deterred. We had the support of our local pastor and Bishop and so we pressed on.

Soon requests came in for radio and TV interviews. At first it was strictly Christian media but soon our efforts attracted the attention of the mainstream media. We accepted them all and held the line as many tried to paint us as fear mongers, radical in our beliefs and threatening to the peace and security of our nation. Through it all we put our complete trust in God as he continually strengthened us to accomplish the mission he had given.

But what happened next was something far beyond anything we could have anticipated. A letter arrived from Rome. We were being summoned to The Vatican!

~

CONGREGATION FOR THE DOCTRINE OF THE FAITH

Letter to Christina and Jennifer Markus

(October 13, 2016)

Dear Christina and Jennifer,

The Congregation for the Doctrine of the Faith, on the 99th anniversary of the Miracle of the Sun at Fatima, has noted with the greatest attention the three pamphlets authored by you which were sent to us under the date of October 13, 2015. In response to your claims expressed in the pamphlets, the Congregation thanks you for the details you have provided. The Congregation wishes to convey to you its feelings in these matters.

1. The Congregation first of all takes note of your declarations regarding the visions of Pope Leo XIII, Pope Saint Pius X and the three children of Fatima. While we appreciate your enthusiasm regarding these private revelations, we shall leave their interpretation to divine providence.

2. We agree with your assertions regarding the Prayer to Saint Michael and its discontinuance following the Second Vatican Council. However, for many dioceses around the world, this prayer has seen resurgence in recent years and in these places, it has been restored to its rightful place at the conclusion of the daily Mass. We leave it for each diocese to make the judgment as to whether they will once again include this most venerable prayer as a daily practice.

3. The dangers of Freemasonry have been addressed in great detail over the centuries by our venerable brother Popes and Cardinals. Many of the faithful have expressed genuine concerns about its influence over the current makeup of the hierarchy of the Church but the Congregation wishes to assure you and all of the faithful that such concerns are overstated and pose no imminent threat to the Magisterium or to the very foundation of the Mystical Body of Christ.

4. The Holy Sacrifice of the Mass is certainly under attack by the secular media and is a constant source of ridicule for those outside the Church that intentionally misrepresent its true meaning. But the Congregation is emphatic in its declaration that the Church

considers that primary to the Liturgy of the Eucharist in the Holy Sacrifice of the Mass is and will always be the representation of the infinite and perfect offering of Our Savior on Calvary to the Glory of God the Father through the power of the Holy Spirit for the expiation of sin. Once again the Congregation wishes to assure you and all of the faithful that any and all evidence to the contrary is patently false and without merit.

5. Regarding the appearance of the Antichrist, the Congregation concedes the existence of certain signs appearing in the world today that indicate the possible close proximity to his entrance onto the world's stage. However, we must also warn against sensationalizing these future events and causing unnecessary fear and disturbance to the lives of the faithful.

In closing, given the concerns expressed here, the Congregation requests that you cease from distributing your pamphlets to any and all locations both inside and outside of the boundaries of your local diocese until such time that we are able to meet with you privately to discuss our recommendations.

Given the courageous display of your faith and equally your concern for the propagation and protection of the faith, the Congregation wishes to invite you to Vatican City and be our guests on May 13, 2017 as the Church celebrates the 100th anniversary of the apparitions of Our Blessed Mother Mary at Fatima. We can schedule to meet with you during your stay here and explore options for modification of the details put forth in your booklets.

If you so desire to accept our invitation, we can make arrangements for you to arrive on Thursday, May 11 of next year and stay at the Casa di Accoglienza Paolo VI on the edge of the Vatican. We look forward to your timely response to our request.

Finally, the Congregation wishes to inform you of our intentions to publish this letter, accompanied, if it so please God, by your act of adherence to our wishes.

Please accept the expression of our sentiments of respectful devotion in the Lord.

Cardinal Francesco Trovina

Prefect

Archbishop Andrea Placare

Secretary

"These guys are afraid of us!" Jenny said out of frustration.

"Or at least afraid of the information we are putting out there."

"They need to silence us just as others have been silenced before us because it exposes their plans to compromise the faith."

"Then they must be hoping that people don't read too deeply into their explanations because their objections don't make much sense. Why would God present visions to two Popes and then to three children at Fatima if he did not want us to comprehend their meaning?" I asked.

"And do they really expect us to accept their word that Freemasonry does not pose a threat from within the Church simply because they've said so?"

"Right, especially considering we have approved private revelation that directly contradicts their claim."

"The same is true for the changing of the Mass. And do we avoid talking about the Antichrist just because it may disturb someone?"

"So what do we do now?"

Jenny paused and thought for a moment.

"We exhibit what we've been praying for; the strength, perseverance and courage of Our Lord. We go to Rome and we make our case."

"That's suicidal!"

"Maybe, but remember, Judas was only one person."

"What is that supposed to mean?"

"Those within the Church that have betrayed the faith and are opposed to our efforts to expose the truth about their plans to destroy the faith are in power for sure, but they are few in number; just as Judas was only one of twelve. There must be many other good Priests, Bishops and Cardinals in the Vatican that from behind the scenes can help us expose these dangers and warn the faithful."

"But how do we find them?"

"Look, we can see the ongoing battle already taking place in the media. We have Cardinal versus Cardinal and Bishop verses Bishop debating openly on the changes that are being proposed. It's easy to see which Cardinals and Bishops are resisting these changes and which ones are pushing for them. These faithful are the ones that we petition for help."

And so we did. We sent letters along with our pamphlets to the offices of three Cardinals and nine Bishops residing in the Vatican, all of whom were clear in their defense of the faith. We made our case and asked for their help and support, informing them of our plans to accept the invitation extended to us and travel to Rome for the 100th anniversary of Fatima.

Nine weeks later, we received a letter from one of the Cardinals, Cardinal Giuseppe Tutore, pledging his help in reversing the decision of The Congregation for the Doctrine of the Faith. He even extended an offer to meet with him at his office in the Vatican along with three of the nine Bishops we petitioned, on the day after we arrive, Friday, May 12. We quickly accepted his offer.

Despite their vehement claims to the contrary, in early 2017, discussions did begin within the Vatican and with prominent heads of different Protestant denominations to change the essentials of the Mass so that all Christians could unite under a single worship service. The heated debate that followed within the Church raged over the next few months with conservative Cardinals holding the line against vicious attacks from the liberal contingent claiming that the conservative wing was blocking the historic re-unification of all Christians. As we boarded the plane to Rome later that May, the fulfillment of the Fatima prophecies loomed large.

~

"Ladies and gentlemen, the Captain has turned on the Fasten Seat Belt sign. If you haven't already done so, please stow your carry-on luggage underneath the seat in front of you or in an overhead bin. Please take your seat and fasten your seat belt. Make sure your seat and folding trays are in their full upright positions. At this time, we request that all cell phones be turned off for the full duration of the flight, as these might interfere with the navigational and communication equipment on this aircraft."

"Well, here we go. Did you remember to bring the original letter from The Congregation for the Doctrine of the Faith, so that we can show it to Cardinal Tutore?"

"Yes." I said. "And I also brought Father Mike's journal so that he could examine that as well."

"Do you think that's a good idea? If that's misplaced or worse stolen, we lose our primary source of information."

"C'mon, I'm not that stupid. I have a soft copy. But we need to show the Cardinal Father Mike's actual journal in order to give our story some credibility."

"I don't disagree with that but it's still risky. That's 25 years worth of research you're holding in your hot little hands there."

"Don't worry; I'll be sure to keep it with me wherever we go."

"Please do. By the way, I checked out the place where we're staying."

"What's it like?"

"The accommodations are modest but it looks comfortable. What's nice is that it's right on the edge of the Vatican. We can walk to everywhere we have to be. When I was an exchange student, we lived only about 3 blocks from this place, so I know the area real well."

"How close are we to where we have to meet Cardinal Tutore tomorrow?"

"It's maybe a ten minute walk, right across Saint Peter's Square. And then on Saturday afternoon on the 13th, the festivities for the 100th anniversary celebration of Fatima will take place right in the square."

"Oh that's perfect. And when do we meet again with the representatives of The Congregation for the Doctrine of the Faith?" I asked.

"Also on the 13th, but at 9AM, long before the celebration begins."

"That'll be a bit scary."

"Yeah, but I'm hoping that Cardinal Tutore along with the other three Bishops we are meeting with tomorrow can prep us for the meeting and give us some sound advice on how to respond to the congregation's demands to change the content of the pamphlets."

"Do we know the names of the other three Bishops? Yeah, I put them in the itinerary I wrote up."

"Man, you are organized."

"Someone has to be. I knew I couldn't count on you. Ok, the three Bishops are Bishop Daniel Taylor from England, Bishop Miguel Santos from Portugal and Bishop Giovanni Romano from Italy."

"Right, I remember those names from when we were looking for Bishops and Cardinals in the Vatican that were defenders of the faith and that we could petition for support."

"Well according to the letter we received from Cardinal Tutore, they all read the pamphlets and according to his words, they found nothing contrary to the faith. In fact he said they found the information 'accurate and timely'."

"That should mean that they currently see present in the Vatican the dangers that we warn about."

"I should think so. But I guess we're gonna find out."

"By the way, I did something that should be a pleasant surprise to you." I confessed.

"Oh great, is this another one of your Nancy Drew things?"

"Not exactly."

"Wait, let me brace myself."

"About a month ago, I sent a copy of the letter we received from The Congregation for the Doctrine of the Faith to Father Ramos, along with copies of our pamphlets. I also told him about our trip to Rome, our meeting with Cardinal Tutore and the scheduled meeting with representatives from The Congregation."

"Nice! Did you hear back from him?"

"Yeah, I received a letter back from him about a week ago."

"What did he say?"

"He said that he was really proud of us and the pamphlets were an excellent idea and well done. He said that Cardinal Tutore was a great guardian of the faith and that we should let him guide us every step of the way. He assured us of his prayers and he gave us his cell phone number. He wants us to text him after our meeting with the good Cardinal and then again after we meet with The Congregation. He said to be very careful, that we are sheep in the midst of wolves and we must pray constantly for Our Lord and his Blessed Mother to direct our every step. He also said to pray the Prayer to Saint Michael as often as we can."

"That's great advice and we'll be sure to do all of that. It sure is great to hear from him. I've been wondering how he's been doing."

"I like the fact that we can text him if we sense trouble." I said.

"Yeah, I guess he's not so worried about our direct contact anymore."

"Well it was almost two years ago. Things have probably calmed down quite a bit since then."

"I wonder if they ever got to the bottom of Father Mike's mysterious death."

"You know how those things go. I'm sure it was just written off as due to natural causes."

"Yeah, you're probably right."

"Boy that's not something that I hear from you too often."

"Well, you have your moments. Listen, this is a long flight and we might want to get some rest. We got up way too early this morning and by the time we get to Rome; it's going to already be about 6PM. Fortunately, our meeting tomorrow is not until after lunch."

"I'm too wound up. I'm going to watch a few movies."

"Be my guest. Just don't wake me up as you apparently love to do. Feel free to eat my food if they bring us anything. There's great food where we're heading. I'll wait till then. See you in Rome."

"Pleasant dreams, Jenn."

Heading to Rome I couldn't help but contemplate how far we had come. It certainly borders on the miraculous. I mean who would have thought two years ago that at this time of our lives Jenn and I would be issuing warnings to the world about the end times and then subsequently summoned to the Vatican by the hierarchy of the Catholic Church because we were ruffling some feathers. We were just two girls in our early twenties enjoying life and oblivious to the world events around us. Our close proximity to the arrival of the Antichrist was the furthest thing from our minds. And yet here we are. It only proves that you can't fathom what God has in store for those that seek to do his will.

Feeling prompted to pray; I decided to forgo the watching of movies and chose instead to pray for the safety and success of our trip. I prayed all twenty mysteries of the Rosary contemplating the very saving events in the lives of Jesus and Mary; the five Joyful Mysteries, the five Luminous Mysteries, the five Sorrowful Mysteries and the five Glorious Mysteries. I followed that by praying The Chaplet of Divine Mercy, focusing intensely on the sorrowful passion endured by Our Lord for our salvation. I felt God's burning presence inside of me like I had never experienced before. I held on firmly to that feeling as I slowly drifted off into a deep sleep. The next thing I knew, I was awakened by an in-flight passenger announcement that was music to my ears.

~

"Ladies and gentlemen, welcome to Fiumicino International Airport. Local time is 6:05 PM and the temperature is 64 degrees. For your safety and comfort, please remain seated with your seat belt fastened until the Captain turns off the Fasten Seat Belt sign. This will indicate that we have parked at the gate and that it is safe for you to move about. Please check around your seat for any personal belongings you may have brought on board with you and please use caution when opening the overhead bins, as heavy articles may have shifted around during the flight."

"Jenn, wake up. We're here."

"What? We're here already?"

"I know I was passed out too."

"Man, I slept the whole way. That was fantastic! I can't remember when I've slept so soundly."

"Maybe that was just God's way of preparing us for the tough days ahead."

"Well if that's the case, then I wouldn't mind being prepared like that more often."

"Yeah I know; me too." I said as I laughed. "Hey, by the way, how are we getting from here to the place where we're staying?"

"It's easy. We just take the train into Rome and grab a taxi from the train station."

"Oh ok, then I guess we'll need to exchange some dollars."

"Right, we'll do that here in the airport after picking up our luggage and getting through customs. Let's get going. The line is starting to move."

~

Once through customs we headed for the currency exchange. Riding up an escalator and reaching the top, there was a team of security nearby that was stopping people from making their way across the corridor and into the entrance of the exchange. We were being held back while an entourage of people entered the airport and made their way to the security entrance and down to their departure gate. There had to be at least 50 to 60 people in the entourage. They must be accompanying a celebrity, famous politician or someone of great importance.

"Great, that's all we need is more delays. I haven't eaten anything in like 12 hours." Jenny said out of frustration. "And who is this guy that they're surrounding?"

"I can't tell. He doesn't look familiar. Nobody else seems to recognize him either."

I glanced at Jenny and she suddenly froze. Her face turned ashen white as if in horror.

"What's wrong?"

"It's him!!" She whispered emphatically.

"It's who?"

"It's him!! It's the Antichrist!!"

"Luther?"

"Yes!!"

I quickly looked to my left as he began to walk past; everything seemed to move in slow motion. He looked to be about 5' 8" tall, approximately 165 lbs with medium length black hair and a square shaped face. He had that same Asian look that we saw so many times in pictures we pulled down from the Internet. He was noticeably older now, more mature. He was wearing a purple and white, full-length cassock with a solid purple sash that extended from his left shoulder across his chest past his right hip. He wore black and red embroidered leather sandals, with straps across the base of his toes and around his ankles. As he approached closer to where we were standing, he suddenly focused his gaze upon us, staring us down. As he slowly strolled past, his head turned to continue his intense scrutiny as if he knew who we were. His eyes were like a doll's eyes, lifeless, black and empty as if he had no soul. With a devious smile he nodded as if to acknowledge "game on", the battle is now joined. Now well past, he returned his focus to once again look straight ahead. Jenny continued to gape at him as he melded into a sea of activity.

"How did you become aware so quickly that it was him?" I asked half confused.

"I heard the voice of Jesus within me just like before."

"What did he say?"

"He said, 'BEHOLD, THE BEAST.'"

"Wow! This is all just so incredible!"

"That was meant to happen." Jenny said still looking numb from the encounter.

"How do you know that?"

"I just know. It was important for us to encounter him and see him leaving Rome. And his seeing us was God's way of letting him know that his identity had been revealed to us."

"He sure looked like he knew who we were. And what was he doing in Rome?"

"No doubt he was making preparations."

"Making preparations for what?"

"Remember what was said at La Salette; 'Rome will lose the faith and become the seat of the Antichrist'."

"Right, and the False Prophet, his partner, a Cardinal in the Vatican, will assist with his deceptive plans."

"Precisely; it could very well be that given the 100th Anniversary of Fatima on Saturday, something is already in the works. And his leaving town might be evidence of that. He greases the rails and leaves the dirty work for others so that later he can ride in on a white horse to bring peace and save the day. Always remember that dates matter. We have already seen evidence of that."

"All the more reason for us to be wary of the circumstances we may find ourselves exposed to this weekend."

"And as we have already surmised, his first public appearance may be less than 7 months away."

"So he may have been in Rome making his final preparations."

"I'm afraid so. C'mon, let's get to the exchange. We still have to catch a train into Rome and then a taxi to the house. We'll talk more about this over dinner."

As each day passes, I am more and more amazed at the courage Jenny displays. From the very beginning she was always the reluctant one. Now she is the stronger one, determined not to back down, even in the face of pure evil; an evil which the world has never known and which will take it by complete surprise.

By the time we settled into our room, it was almost 9PM. Fortunately for us, most of the locals don't eat their dinner until about this time, so there were many restaurants to choose from. Jenny had her favorite all picked out, so we quickly scrambled from our room, walking the 5 blocks to quell our hunger.

~

"So we can take our time, have a good long meal and sleep in tomorrow because our meeting with Cardinal Tutore and the three Bishops is not until after lunch, right around 2PM." Jenny explained.

"That sounds good. I have to tell you, though; I'm still freaked out from what just happened back there at the airport. We just came face to face with the Bible's "Man of Iniquity", "Son of Perdition", "Lawless One", the "Beast"; the actual Antichrist that scholars have searched for millennia to discover, and we came within a few feet of him and didn't cower."

"We have to come to grips with the fact that things will continue to move in our direction. God is directing our steps and so being on the front lines will become commonplace. But we won't be alone. We have to remember that when we stand, we stand with Heaven's legions. And that makes us stronger than our enemies can possibly imagine."

"I've got to tell you, each day I am more and more convinced that the few words that Jesus spoke to you imparted within you not just his words but also his wisdom, his courage, his strength and his perseverance, along with a supernatural sense that I just do not possess."

"I know. I do sense these changes and I suspect that they have been given for a reason. We have to expose what these guys are up to. Failure is not an option."

"Oh I agree. But it's just so inspiring to see you stand so strong in the face of pure evil."

"We have no choice. We were given a mission and with God's help, we will accomplish it. That's the attitude we must have."

"I'm with you."

"Ok this place has great food and I'm starved, so let's relax and enjoy this because these next few days may be a little hectic."

We did just that and stayed for a good three hours. There's a reason why Italy is known for their food. We don't have Italian restaurants back home that can compete with this cuisine. And when the home grown wine hits your palate, it's as though you can taste the very soil that nurtured the grapes.

"Didn't I tell you how good these restaurants were?"

"That was amazing." I said. "I can't imagine being able to eat like this every day. I could get used to this."

"And that's why I loved it so much when I lived here."

"What's not to love?"

"That's precisely how I feel. Now you know why when I returned home, I told Mom and Dad that I wanted to come back to live here for a few years."

"Yeah, I remember Dad saying you were crazy. I guess I'm beginning to appreciate your point of view."

"Thank you. Finally someone gets it."

"I guess we should start heading back. It's after midnight. I hope the streets are safe around here."

"Are you kidding? We're on the edge of the Vatican. These are some of the safest streets in all of Italy."

"And I hope those beds are comfortable."

"They are. I checked them out. They're nice and firm, so no back-aches." Jenny said with a smile.

The Casa di Accoglienza Paolo VI was a nice comfortable 3-story home, run by Catholic nuns. It looked to have about 12 rooms. There were very pretty fenced-in court yards and inside there were marble floors and high ceilings. The rooms were simple and clean with every-thing you needed. Rooftop lounge areas overlooked the quaint, peace-ful streets below and made for nice resting spots. Everything was neat and orderly.

But all of that was in stark contrast to what we were about to dis-cover. Upon returning to our room we were shocked to find the con-tents of our luggage dumped on the floor. Mattresses and box springs were flipped over and tossed aside. The drawers in both bureaus were fully extended and the closet doors had been flung open. The window overlooking the courtyard was left open.

"What the frig!!" Jenny yelled in frustration.

"Oh man! Our stuff is everywhere."

"Who would do this?"

"And what were they looking for?"

"Wait, I'll bet I know what they were looking for."

"What?"

And then we both said in unison.

"The Journal!"

"Chrissy, please tell me you still have it."

"I told you that I would carry it with me wherever we went. It's right here in my bag."

"Well that's good. But how would they even know about it. We didn't mention anywhere or to anyone that Father Mike's Journal was the source for the information in the pamphlets."

"Oh yes we did."

"Where and to whom?"

"We showed it to our pastor and our local Bishop, remember?"

"Oh yeah, we did. We did it so our story would have the credibility we needed to get their permission to distribute the pamphlets within the parish and then across the diocese."

"That's right."

"So why would they sell us out?"

"No, I'm sure they didn't. Think about it. Since we were being summoned, it's probably customary for the Vatican to contact our local pastor and Bishop and inform them of their request. They were probably asked if we had approached them and if so, what did we tell them?"

"So if they confiscate the original journal they would have all of Father Mike's research and from their perspective, we would lose credibility since what we present in the pamphlets could be cast as just the ramblings of two inexperienced lay women who have no formal training in Eschatology."

"That's very clever; except for the fact that they would be taking a chance that we have no other hard copy and no soft copy."

"That may be true but there is no better source than the original. If they have that, then they can label anything else we have as not comprehensive."

"That's a strange world they operate in."

"True, but all they need is something they can use to put doubt in the mind of the faithful and then we can be written off as not being credible."

"But first things first, we need to get out of this first floor room and moved preferably to one on the third floor so our room can't be accessed from the courtyard."

We immediately called the caretaker and requested that he come to inspect our room. We explained what had happened and he quickly agreed to move us to a room on the third floor. He said that he saw no one and heard nothing. We were convinced that whoever perpetrated this break-in must have been a professional. Given what we knew about the inner workings of the Vatican, we were still astounded by the apparent nest of intrigue that operates within it.

Having endured more than our daily share of stress filled moments, we settled in for the night. By 9:00 in the morning the activity on the street to and from the nearby museum on the grounds of the Vatican made it almost impossible to sleep any longer. We prepared ourselves for the day and made ourselves comfortable at a nearby café.

⁓

"Maybe I'm paranoid, but there's a guy sitting at a table across the street that hasn't stopped looking in our direction. He's wearing a white T-shirt with blue jeans. Do you see him, Jenn?"

"Yeah I see him. This is like something out of a James Bond movie. Make sure you hang on tight to the bag that has our stuff."

"Oh believe me, I will."

"So as I mentioned, the offices of Cardinal Tutore are located just on the other side of Saint Peter's square. So we should give ourselves about 30 minutes to get there in plenty of time given that the crowds will be fairly large by that time of day."

"That sounds good. I have several copies of the pamphlets and of course Father Mike's Journal. Is there anything else we need?"

"No, that should be it. We may as well hang here until about 12:30 and then we can head back to our room and get ready to leave."

"And we should pray the Rosary before we leave!" I insisted.

"I know, I know, I didn't forget. And let's keep an eye on spy man over there."

We returned to our room without any indication of being followed. As planned, at 1:30 we headed out into Saint Peter's Square. Preparations were being made for the celebration the next day, so we did have some difficulty walking around the roped off areas in order to access the main part of the plaza. We then made our way across to the other side, past the obelisk and down the road where Cardinal Tutore was located. It was my first time walking through Saint Peter's Square, so Jenny narrated the amazing history of the sites along the way.

The 3 story building where the Cardinal was housed was situated about halfway down Via della Conciliazione which connects Saint Peter's Square to Castel Sant'Angelo, a huge cylindrical shaped building operating as a hotel and located on the west bank of the Tiber River. It was commissioned by the Roman Emperor Hadrian in 123 A.D. as a mausoleum for himself and his family. I so wish we had more time to explore these sites. I had to constantly catch myself from getting too lost in the awesome history of my surroundings and forgetting that we had a serious job to do. Entering the Cardinal's residence you couldn't help but be impressed by the beauty of the marble floors, high decorative ceilings and impressive artwork. The attractive features of this place helped to soothe our nervousness. We arrived about 10 minutes early and were greeted by a pleasant looking, well-dressed woman about 50 years of age.

"Hello, may I help you?" She said speaking in slightly broken English.

"Yes, my name is Christina Markus and this is my sister Jennifer. We are here to see Cardinal Tutore."

"Yes, he is expecting you. Please follow me. Have you ladies ever had the pleasure of meeting with a Cardinal before?"

"No we haven't." I said.

"Well there is no reason to be nervous but you should address the good Cardinal as your Eminence. His brother Bishops you simply address as Bishop."

"Thank you. We'll be sure to remember that."

"They're waiting for you both in here and remember, don't be nervous." She whispered and smiled as she opened the door."

As we entered the spacious room we saw the Cardinal and his three brother Bishops seated at the right end of a large boardroom worthy conference table with the Cardinal at the head of the table and the three Bishops to his right. They all stood and approached us with warm smiles.

"Hello Christina and Jennifer. My name is Cardinal Tutore." He said in broken English.

"Your Eminence, it's so nice to meet you." I said shaking his hand. "And this is my sister, Jennifer."

"Hello Jennifer, welcome."

"Your Eminence, it's nice to meet you."

"These are my brother Bishops, Bishop Miguel Santos from Portugal, Bishop Daniel Taylor from England and Bishop Giovanni Romano from right here in Italy."

"It's nice to meet you Bishop." Jenny and I said shaking hands with each of the Bishops.

"Please have a seat and make yourselves comfortable. Would you like some water or something else to drink?" The Cardinal asked.

"No thank you." We both said taking our seats.

We took seats opposite the Bishops and to the left of Cardinal Tutore. The Cardinal began.

"Well, you ladies have caused quite a stir here at the Vatican. But we consider it a good thing." He said with a smile. "We liked your pamphlets."

"Thank you. That's comforting to hear." I said.

"Would you ladies mind telling us how this all started?" Bishop Taylor asked.

Jenny and I looked at each other and Jenny motioned for me to start.

"Jenny and I were on vacation with our family in Tacoma, Washington two years ago in June of 2015. Our Uncle is a club Golf Professional and that year he qualified for the US Open Golf Championship at Chambers Bay Golf Club just outside of Tacoma. So we were all there to see him play for the first time in the US Open. Our parents rented a house in Tacoma for the week and while there I came across this obscure journal in a kitchen drawer."

I placed Father Mike's journal on the table and pushed it gently towards Cardinal Tutore who picked it up and began to page through it.

"I showed it to my sister Jenny and seeing that the journal belonged to a Father Michael Thomas, we attempted to return it to him at his parish in Wisconsin only to find that Father Michael had been found dead in the parking lot of a Church close to where we were staying. Father Michael was staying in the very same house we rented when he met his untimely death. We found a letter in the journal from Father Michael to his friend, Father Daniel Ramos who was a parish priest also close by in Tacoma, Washington. Not knowing where else to go with Father Michael's journal, we met with Father Ramos to offer it to him. He explained that Father Michael was a good friend of his from back in Divinity School and had spent 25 years researching public and private revelation. This research led him to conclude that not only were we living in the end times but that critical end time prophecy was about to unfold. He said that Father Michael's research pointed specifically to a major betrayal that was about to befall the Mystical Body of Christ, the Church, just as Judas betrayed Jesus which lead to the passion and death of the physical Body of Christ. Father Ramos explained that there was a parallel between the suffering of the physical Body of Christ and the current suffering being experienced by the Mystical Body of Christ. Father Ramos told us that he was assisting at a US Bishops Conference in Tacoma the week that Father Michael died. Father Ramos had worked with Father Michael to have a summary of his work placed in the Bishops packets to warn the Bishops of this impending betrayal. The summary was approved by the chief moderator for the conference but was subsequently removed from the packets before the Bishops convened. Father Michael was found dead the next day. Father Ramos was concerned that the visiting Cardinal who flew in from Rome attending as a Vatican observer may have had something to do with both stopping the distribution of the summary and the mysterious death of Father Michael. Thinking that he might place himself in grave danger if he took possession of the journal, Father Ramos encouraged Jenny and me to study Father Mike's research on our own to see if we could find a way to bring the truth he discovered to the faithful and to the world. After much soul searching and prayer, we decided to accept the challenge. After spending 3 months studying the journal and researching the topics, we determined that the best course of action would be to summarize the most important details of his thesis into a series of pamphlets. And so we did, and subsequently these pamphlets caused all the commotion."

"Why did Father Ramos feel that the Cardinal attending the Bishops Conference as the Vatican observer may have had something to do with the removal of the summary and the death of Father Michael?" Cardinal Tutore asked.

"Father Ramos told us that other than the Bishop moderator, the visiting Cardinal was the only other person aware of both the summary and the identity of its author."

"Was the summary the only contact that Father Michael was to have with the Bishops?" Bishop Santos inquired.

"No. Father Ramos said that the plan was to have Father Michael address the Bishops with a presentation of the topics discussed in the summary once the Bishops had finished their scheduled order of business. He requested this of both the Bishop moderator as well as the attending Cardinal."

"And why was Father Ramos concerned for his own safety if he chose to continue Father Michael's work?" Bishop Taylor asked.

"Father Ramos indicated to us that because the research pointed to an imminent deception from within the highest levels of the Church and because he himself had taken a vow of obedience, it would just be a matter of time before he would either be silenced by his superiors or worse; possibly suffer the same fate as Father Michael. And so he felt that the best chance of success was to have us expose it."

"Well you certainly have succeeded in doing that and at the same time attract quite a bit of attention from the hierarchy." Cardinal Tutore said with a smile. "You see Christina and Jennifer, we feel as Father Michael discovered through private revelation that the Church is about to be plunged into a sea of changes of which there is no return. We see it based on our close proximity to the discussions that are currently taking place. We are doing our best to fight these battles from the inside but we are beginning to feel that the tide is turning against us. So we want to assist however we can with your efforts to expose this truth from the outside."

"We certainly don't want you to change the content of your pamphlets in any way." Bishop Romano added. "This is what the Congregation for the Doctrine of the Faith will attempt to force you to do. As you may suspect, we feel that the enemy that Father Michael's research warns about, lies within the Congregation."

"There may be about twenty of them in total within the Vatican that are in key positions and are plotting to implement these changes we speak about. But their most powerful elements can be found within the Congregation." Cardinal Tutore indicated. "So understanding that, we would like to prepare you both for what you can expect tomorrow when you meet with the Congregation for the Doctrine of the Faith. They will begin with small talk and smiles, making you feel that you are among friends. You are not. You will be sheep in the midst of wolves. Never forget that. Their goal will be to completely shut your work down. Don't think for one minute that they will accept some slight modifications. They will accept only your adherence to their wishes, which is for you to go home and never think about any of this again."

"Then how can we possibly succeed against such a coordinated force of Church authority?" Jenny asked intently with a sense of frustration.

"You tell them what they want to hear." Bishop Taylor suggested. "You say that you will no longer participate with the distribution of these pamphlets. You have a private publisher do you not?"

"Yes we do." I said.

"And is that publisher affiliated in any way with the Catholic Church?" Bishop Taylor continued.

"No, as a matter of fact the owner is Jewish."

"Then you simply tell the publisher to remove your names from further printings and allow the orders to come in and the publisher to fill those orders. You stay out of the process. You have done your work. You just let it continue unabated. And in the process you remain true to your word." Bishop Taylor concluded. "At that point they can't touch you and they have no authority over the inner workings of a private business."

"That's brilliant!" Jenny added.

"Hopefully that should ease your minds?" Cardinal Tutore asked.

"Yes; very much so." I said.

"Fine, I'm glad we were able to help." Cardinal continued. "Before you both leave, I'd like to give you a feel for the logistics of your meeting tomorrow. The moderator will be a Cardinal Santiago Boguilegro."

Jenny and I quickly turned to make eye contact as the blood rushed from our faces. We both instantaneously recalled that Cardinal Boguilegro was the Vatican observer that Father Ramos told us he suspected may have been responsible for the mysterious death of Father Michael. Not recognizing our reaction, Cardinal Tutore continued speaking.

"He will be accompanied by about 8 others, some of which will be Cardinals and Bishops, and others priests."

"Wait!" I yelled.

"What's wrong?" The Cardinal asked.

"Cardinal Boguilegro was the Vatican observer at the Bishops Conference in Tacoma. He's the one that Father Ramos suspected had something to do with the death of his friend."

"May God have Mercy!" Bishop Romano exclaimed.

"He may be the kingpin we have been trying to identify after all." Bishop Santos added.

"And it was only recently that he was promoted to the Congregation." The Cardinal recalled.

"And nominated to be their media spokesperson where he gives very liberal interpretations of Church doctrine, causing so much confusion." Bishop Taylor interjected.

"If he is the kingpin and if Father Michael's analysis is correct, then Cardinal Boguilegro may in fact be the Biblical False Prophet that we surmised was indeed within our midst." The Cardinal explained to his brother Bishops.

"Daniel's 'Roman Prince'." Bishop Romano declared in broken English while shaking his head in disgust.

Jenny and I sat in amazement as all four discussed the possibility that Cardinal Boguilegro is actually the False Prophet, the one the Prophet Daniel and John the Apostle warned would precede the Antichrist.

"My brother Bishops, given these circumstances, we cannot in good conscience allow these two to walk into a meeting with these wolves in sheep's clothing."

The good Cardinal thought for a moment and then proposed the following.

"Jennifer and Christina, with your permission, I will write a letter to the Congregation on your behalf requesting that your pamphlets be given to three of the Church's top theologians asking them to act as censors to judge whether the pamphlets contain content in any way that would harm correct faith or good morals. If they judge the content of the pamphlets as free of doctrinal and moral error, then the Congregation would be hard pressed to ban them or even ask that the content be modified. If they judge them as containing content that would harm correct faith, then I will assure them that you will adhere to the wishes of the Congregation, whatever those wishes might be. If the result is the latter, then we can continue with the approach that we discussed previously where your names are removed. They will have to respect your wishes to have the pamphlets evaluated by an independent, competent Church authority as it is well within your rights to do so. This will tie their hands at least temporarily and will give us a chance to nullify their attempts to silence you. This move will surprise them and be an indication that you will not be bullied. With your permission I will have this letter completed within the hour and hand delivered to Cardinal Boguilegro."

"Your Eminence, that sounds wonderful. We sincerely appreciate your assistance with this." I said.

"As I say, we are happy to assist wherever we can. We are all so proud of you both for the work you are doing. Stay strong and persevere in the faith and know that there are many of us that support you. Now my dear children please go in peace and without any fear. And please allow us to extend to you our blessings."

The Cardinal and Bishops spoke the blessing in unison.

"May the blessing of Almighty God, the Father, the Son and the Holy Spirit descend upon you and remain with you forever."

"Amen." Jenny and I responded as we felt a penetrating heat descend upon us.

We said our goodbyes and left the good Cardinal's residence elated that the following morning we would not have to face the grilling of the Congregation for the Doctrine of the Faith.

"Did you feel that?" I asked Jenny.

"Yeah, my body temperature felt like it was about 110 degrees."

"That's exactly how I felt."

"I'll bet it's like a defensive shield that no evil can penetrate."

"I really believe that."

"I know me too."

"And what a relief it is that we don't have to face the Congregation."

"We would have been lambs for slaughter if not for Cardinal Tutore."

"Any doubt he was sent by Heaven to intercede for us?"

"I have no doubt at all."

Leaving the building we decided to head back to our room to relax and reflect on what had just transpired.

"When we get back to the room, we have to remember to text Father Ramos and let him know how it went with Cardinal Tutore." I said. "I'm sure he'll be thrilled to hear how the Cardinal rescued us from almost certain defeat."

"I suspect he will be."

Jenny paused slightly to look over her shoulder.

"By the way, don't look now but 007 is back."

"I thought that was him." I said without looking. "He's across the street and pretty much step for step with us."

"That's him. You'd think he'd at least change his clothes so as not to be so obvious."

"We should walk directly at him and confront him."

"Given where we are, and who we're up against, I think it might be best to lay low and not put ourselves in any more danger."

"But I'd sure like to know who sent him."

"I think this means we may want to be real careful tomorrow."

We grabbed some food and drink on the way back so we could have dinner in our room to avoid further intrigue. We were followed all the way back to the house. Upon entering, we watched out the window as our boy disappeared into a crowd.

"So what do we do if he's back out following us again tomorrow?" I asked.

"We ignore him as best we can and we enjoy the celebration. We'll be leaving on Monday and so we lay low until we're in the air. I never thought I'd say that about a place I love so much but we are clearly not very safe over here."

"I'm going to text Father Ramos the details of our meeting today. He'll be happy to hear that we won't be facing the Congregation tomorrow."

"But that's only a temporary reprieve. I'm sure he'll understand that. We have to hope and pray that we're not summoned back here again sometime in the near future."

"But even if we are, at least we now know we have powerful allies that will stand with us."

"True. But even they can be pushed aside by those in more powerful positions."

"In the meantime we can continue our work. Oh I forgot to tell you that I received an email from our publisher and he said the requests for the pamphlets are going through the roof. He said he received big orders from folks in South Carolina, Florida and Texas."

"The Holy Spirit is clearly taking over."

"That's what happens when we simply do our part."

"Speaking of that, we have to start thinking about getting them translated into other languages before we get shut down. This is way too important to include only those that speak English and Spanish. Let's make that a priority when we get back."

"I agree. Hey I'm going to send out this text message."

"I'll get the food ready. Let's eat out on the third floor terrace. We'll be safe up there."

~

Father Ramos responded immediately after receiving my text. He was clearly pleased with the outcome of the meeting and he reiterated to trust Cardinal Tutore and allow him to guide our every step. He reassured us of his prayers for our safe return and he counseled us to be very wary of our surroundings at all times.

"I already said grace for the both of us. So what did he mean about being very wary of our surroundings at all times? Did you tell him about spy man?"

"No." I said. "I didn't want him to worry. Can you pass me a napkin?"

"He must know how these things go down. I'm starting to wonder about whether we should even go back to the square for the celebration."

"But this will be historic."

"I know but it just doesn't feel right. I'd like to get home in one piece. I guess we can make that call after we get up in the morning."

"That works for me. Let's stop worrying about that for now and enjoy our food. I want to relax tonight. It's been a long day."

"Ok, you have my word, no more talk about anything stressful for the rest of the night."

After finishing our dinner and while still relaxing on the outdoor terrace, we once again looked to the heavens and recited our calling card prayer for strength. But somehow sitting here in Rome just steps from the Vatican and Saint Peter's Basilica, it seemed to have so much more significance and felt so much more powerful.

"Eternal God, in whom mercy is endless and the treasury of compassion inexhaustible, look kindly upon us and increase Your mercy in us, that in difficult moments we might not despair nor become despondent, but with great confidence submit ourselves to Your holy will, which is Love and Mercy itself. Amen."

CHAPTER 11

PROPHECY FULFILLED

"Chrissy! You forgot to turn the ringer off on your phone."

"What?" I said half asleep.

"I said you forgot to turn the ringer off on your phone. You've gotten like 10 text messages in the last 5 minutes and it's really annoying."

"What time is it?"

"It's 3 AM. Turn the stupid phone off."

I glanced at my phone and was mortified at what I saw.

"You've got to be freaking kidding me!" I screamed.

"Now what?"

"The text messages are from Mom and Dad and also from Father Ramos."

"That's a weird combination. Have they forgotten that we are 6 and 9 hours ahead of them?"

"Jenny, Rome is under attack!! They're watching it live on the news."

"Shut up!!"

"I'm not kidding."

"Oh crap!! I can here gunfire. We got to get out of here. What are they saying?"

"Father Ramos says that Islamic forces are attacking along the shores near Fiumicino and have taken over the airport and some have already reached the Vatican. He also says that Russian forces are attacking from the east. They are coming in from the Adriatic and through Lanciano."

"IT'S THE PROPHECY!!" Jenny screamed. "It's the fulfillment of the visions of Pope Leo XIII, Pope Pius X and of the first part of the third secret of Fatima given to the children! It's taking place 100 years to the day of the first apparition at Fatima. Remember I told you that dates have meaning. The miracle of the sun took place exactly 33 years to the day later from when Pope Leo XIII had his vision before the Tabernacle. And he was told about the hundred years and so was Lucia!"

"Everyone is telling us to leave everything and get out now."

"We are living through the Prophecy!" Jenny said in a panicked voice.

"Jenny, calm down; we are getting out right now! Put on the most comfortable clothes you can find and wear your sneakers! We're going to have to make a run for it. Don't forget your passport, your wallet and your money."

"There's a train station just northeast of here but we're going to have to cut through the square if we want to get there fast."

"That'll have to do. Jesus and Mary watch over us. Let's go!"

As we hurried down the stairs, people were scrambling in every direction, screaming and crying. We ran out the door, Jenny in front with me close behind. She knew exactly where to go. As we sprinted through the square, the scene was so horrible that we had to keep looking away. It appeared as though the invading forces were targeting anyone with a clerical collar. The square was strewn with dead bodies of priests. Passing the obelisk and reaching Via della Conciliazione, I noticed a body lying face down on the walkway dressed in scarlet attire like that of a Cardinal. The biretta on the ground several feet away served as clear evidence that it was indeed a Cardinal and that his body must have fallen to the ground abruptly. The body moved slightly as we passed by and I called to Jenny to stop.

"Chrissy, what are you doing? We have to keep moving."

"But it's a Cardinal and I think he's still alive."

"But we can't just stop." Jenny said as she reluctantly returned to where I was.

"Just help me turn him over. We may be able to move him to safety."

As we turned him over we were horrified to discover that it was none other than our beloved friend Cardinal Tutore. He had been shot in the chest. His loss of blood was extensive but barely detectable against the scarlet red of his garments.

"Cardinal Tutore, can you hear me?" I said with an amplified voice.

"Christina and Jennifer," He said barely able to speak. "You must leave me; you must run and save yourselves. You still have great work to do. I'm not going to survive this. I know that. But you must persevere. I will offer my sufferings for you. You must persevere and trust in God. Now go."

"But your Eminence, we may be able to save you." Jenny insisted.

"No. Please, you must leave me. I know I'm dying. A Cardinal must always be willing to shed his blood for the life of the Church. You have been chosen by Our Lord to help save his Church and the blood I shed here will be offered to strengthen your efforts. Now please, go with my blessing."

Barely able to lift his arm, his weakened hand touched our foreheads as he murmured his blessing. He motioned for us to leave him as he closed his eyes and allowed his head to drop to one side. As we began to run again, both Jenny and I were drenched in tears. We knew there was nothing we could do.

Advancing no more than a few hundred feet, we could still hear gunshots but the sounds appeared to be originating from where we were heading. We began to question our strategy when suddenly we heard someone to our right yelling our names over and over again in very broken English. When we turned to look, we were alarmed to discover that it was our secret agent friend. Jenny insisted that we keep going and ignore his calls to stop. Catching up to us he pleaded with us to let him help us get to safety. He insisted that we were headed in the wrong direction.

"Jenny, what if he's telling us the truth?" I asked as we slowed to a jog. "Let's hear him out."

Jenny reluctantly agreed, stopped running and began to interrogate him.

"What is your name and why have you been following us these last three days?"

"My name is Angelo. I was sent to protect you from those who may wish to do you harm. But now that Rome is under siege my task has changed. I must now bring you to safety. But time is of the essence. We must not delay."

"Who sent you?" I asked.

"I can't tell you that right now. But soon you will see for yourself. There are plans in place by those that know of the importance of your work, to help you take refuge in a place where you can return home without further incident. Please, trust me and let me take you to safety before it's too late."

"I believe him." I said looking at his eyes for any indication of deception. "I think he's sincere. It feels right."

"At this point, I don't think we have much choice. The most recent gunfire does appear to be coming from the direction we are heading. Ok, let's go."

Angelo took us southeast, backtracking down obscure one way streets that only a local would know. We ran for about 10 minutes until we came to a dark back alley where a blacked out Suburban was parked and running but without any lights turned on. We stopped in our tracks and looked at Angelo a bit nervous and very confused.

"Angelo, where have you taken us?" I asked with an agitated voice.

"Your answer is in that car. Please go now. There is nothing to fear."

The door behind the passenger seat opened and a hand emerged waving for us to enter. We approached with trepidation but upon reaching the car and stepping in; our fears were immediately replaced with awe and reverence, for inside the car was Pope Benedict XVI himself. He was deep in prayer but even still, he smiled at us and welcomed us, even knowing our names. I thought to myself, who are we to experience such privilege.

The Pope looked very frail but did not appear to be injured in any way. His white Papal garments were splattered with blood. No doubt from attending to his brother priests who were cut down by the invading forces. Jenny and I took a seat in the back as the driver turned on the head lights, put the vehicle in drive and began to move slowly down the one way street. My goodness, they were waiting for us. We glanced at one another as we both knew what each was thinking; the prophecies she spoke of back at the house were indeed unfolding. The two visions of Pope Pius X in 1909 and 1914:

> *"'What I have seen is terrifying!' he cried out. 'Will I be the one, or will it be a successor? What is certain is that the Pope will leave Rome and, in leaving the Vatican, he will have to pass over the dead bodies of his priests!'"*

> *"I have seen one of my successors, of the same name, who was fleeing over the bodies of his brethren. He will take refuge in some hiding place; but after a brief respite, he will die a cruel death. Respect for*

God has disappeared from human hearts. They wish to efface even God's memory. This perversity is nothing less than the beginning of the last days of the world."

And then the vision of the three children at Fatima in 1917:

"And we saw in an immense light that is God: 'something similar to how people appear in a mirror when they pass in front of it' a Bishop dressed in White 'we had the impression that it was the Holy Father'. Other Bishops, Priests, men and women Religious going up a steep mountain, at the top of which there was a big Cross of rough-hewn trunks as of a cork-tree with the bark; before reaching there the Holy Father passed through a big city half in ruins and half trembling with halting step, afflicted with pain and sorrow, he prayed for the souls of the corpses he met on his way; having reached the top of the mountain, on his knees at the foot of the big Cross he was killed by a group of soldiers who fired bullets and arrows at him, and in the same way there died one after another the other Bishops, Priests, men and women Religious, and various lay people of different ranks and positions."

These prophecies were no longer just unfolding before our eyes; our lives had become intertwined with them. We were fleeing the Vatican with the Pope!

As the driver slowly worked his way through the back streets of Rome, we were astonished at how easily we were able to advance completely undetected. It was as though Heaven itself was our protector.

The Pope now lifted his head from prayer and motioned for us to come forward and take a seat next to him. The two priests attending to him who were occupying those seats stood to allow us to take their seats as they retreated to ours. He spoke to us.

"My children, this is a dark day for the Church but one that I knew would eventually arrive. When I was elected Pope 12 years ago, I said to my brother Cardinals, 'pray that I will not be forced to flee the Vatican'. I was well aware of the visions of my beloved brother Pope Saint Pius X and of the vision given to the children at Fatima in the third secret. As much as I did not want to acknowledge, I was sure that I was the 'successor, of the same name' to which the good Pope referred. Now that the time has come, my heart is filled with such great sorrow. I have more work to do but my time on God's earth is soon coming to an end. But you my children, you have much work to do. You have been given the daunting task of helping Our Lord prepare the world for his return. You must start with your own country. The Book of Revelation's Huge Red Dragon, atheistic Communism, lead by Russia and China, is rearing its ugly head once again. Ongoing wars in the Middle East will now spread into Europe and give rise to the Antichrist who will introduce a temporary false peace. Our Sacred Mass will be destroyed and all of Christianity will be forced to unite within a false Church worshipping a false Christ, the man of iniquity, the beast, the Antichrist. He along with the Huge Red Dragon will soon dominate Europe. Once they do, they will then look to destroy Israel and take control of your country. You must awaken all people of good will in the United States to turn to God as one and plead for his Mercy, his forgiveness and his help. The values your country is built upon are being stripped away. I have spoken about this many times. 'There are values worth dying for. When this is denied, life has lost its point. This is not only true for the individual; it is true for nations. A nation has a common culture, shared values that justify the commitment of a citizen's life. If such values cease to exist, a nation loses the social cohesion that preserves a community and a way of life. Man needs transcendence.'[83] And so my dear children, you must wake a nation. Gather all who look to the God of Abraham, Isaac and Jacob and unite them in prayer. If you do that, God will dispense his Grace on your great country and the fire of Divine Love will sweep your republic and ignite in the hearts of the indifferent, a desire to stand against this onslaught that is sure to come. I fear your nation may be the last best hope for the Church and for human freedom."

"Holy Father, we will do our best to do God's will." I said still in awe from hearing his powerful words.

"I know you will and you must always remember that with God's help everything is possible. Never lose heart and rest assured of my prayers."

"Thank you Holy Father. We will do as you say."

"Holy Father, where will you go?" Jenny asked.

"I've made plans for some time now. We will be flying to Portugal from Ciampino Airport just southeast of here. You both will be coming with me. From there arrangements will be made to fly you back home. I will travel to Fatima and take up residence there."

"We are so grateful for your help, Holy Father." Jenny continued. "But why go to Fatima?"

"There are many reasons. What did Our Blessed Mother say about Rome to Melanie and Maximin at La Salette in 1846?"

"Rome will lose the faith and become the seat of the Antichrist." I said without hesitation.

"Yes that's right. Rome will no longer be safe. And recall what Sister Lucia revealed in 1952 about Portugal when referring to the third secret of Fatima."

"In Portugal the dogma of the faith will always be preserved." Jenny asserted.

"Yes that's also right. You both know private revelation very well. Outside of Portugal the faith will be tampered with even to the point of changing the Holy Sacrifice of the Mass to be simply a remembrance of the last supper. This will cause a great schism within the Church. Consequently, only the Bishops that maintain the Mass as the Holy Sacrifice will remain valid Bishops. Any Bishop that goes along with the heretical changes will automatically forfeit their position as an Episcopate. Once this happens, I will ask my good faithful Bishops, who will be much fewer in number than before the schism, to join me in Fatima to finally and explicitly consecrate Russia to the Immaculate Heart of Mary precisely according to Our Lady's request. This will be my last official act as Pope."

"*In the end, my Immaculate Heart will triumph. The Holy Father will consecrate Russia to me, and she shall be converted, and a period of peace will be granted to the world.*" Jenny quoted with a somber voice.

"That's right."

Jenny continued. "And Father Gobbi, the founder of the Marian Movement of Priests, was told by Our Lady that on the very day that Pope Saint John Paul II made the Consecration in 1984, not all Bishops welcomed the invitation and so did not participate. This meant that the explicit Consecration of Russia to the Immaculate Heart of Mary according to her requests was not fully accomplished on that day. And then she added that this consecration would be made to her when the bloody events are well on the way to actuality. The bloody events she speaks of started today!"

"Yes, that's right." The Holy Father said again. "Everything will now unfold; both good and evil. It's sobering, I know, but it must happen this way in order for evil to be completely extinguished from the face of the earth. This is why the work you are doing is so important. People must be warned of the imminent danger. They must prepare and they must take a stand against the evil that will be thrust upon them. The saints will be at your side assisting you. Lean on them."

"We will, Holy Father." I promised.

We arrived at Ciampino Airport and were driven onto the tarmac where a plane was already fueled and running. We were whisked away onto the plane where we quickly seated ourselves. Within minutes we were in the air heading for Portugal.

The plane ride was quiet. Jenny and I shed many tears thinking of Cardinal Tutore, the many priests and all those we saw who were martyred on this day. God's mighty hand had rescued us today from the evil that surrounded us. The very thought of everything he had done for us was so overwhelming. Our trust in him had been elevated to a completely new level.

Looking across the aisle, Pope Benedict was once again immersed in prayer. We decided to do the same. With hushed voices we prayed the Rosary together and then recited our signature prayer three times over.

"Eternal God, in whom mercy is endless and the treasury of compassion inexhaustible, look kindly upon us and increase Your mercy in us, that in difficult moments we might not despair nor become despondent, but with great confidence submit ourselves to Your holy will, which is Love and Mercy itself. Amen."

CHAPTER 12

APOSTLES OF THE LAST DAYS

"How long did they say it would take to get to Portugal?" I asked. "They said the flight time was about 2 hours. We should be landing in Lisbon somewhere around 7AM and then they'll probably have a car drive the Pope to Fatima. Fatima is only about 90 miles north of Lisbon."

"And then what are we going to do?"

"I expect that they'll put us on a plane that leaves later today and will take us back home to Maine. There's no sense in us going to Fatima, only to have to be driven right back to Lisbon tomorrow."

"That makes sense. I'm just so sorry we never had the chance to say goodbye to Angelo."

"I know. All along we had him pegged as our adversary and here he turned out to be our protector."

"And he was a good one at that." I said through tears.

"Chrissy, the Pope is motioning for us to come and sit with him."

We immediately unbuckled our seat belts and crossed the isle to where he was sitting. There were two empty seats to his immediate right since he occupied the window seat. I sat closest to him and spoke first.

"Yes, Holy Father?"

"I wanted to explain to you both that my assistant will remain behind with you in the Lisbon airport while I am driven to Fatima. He will arrange for a flight to bring you home. I want you to know how proud I am of you for having the courage to speak the truth. Never be fearful to speak the truth no matter what the circumstances may be."

"Thank you, Holy Father; we will commit ourselves to that."

"Holy Father," Jenny began. "Christina and I were just discussing how thankful we are to you for sending Angelo to watch over us and protect us and then to bring us to you. But we are so saddened by the fact that we didn't have a chance to thank him or even say goodbye."

"I'm sorry, who is Angelo?" The Holy Father asked.

Jenny and I looked at each other completely perplexed.

"Didn't you send him to look after us?" Jenny asked still looking confused.

"No, I don't know who you are referring to."

"He's a guy that was following us these last three days. We thought all along that we should avoid him because of his seemingly dubious behavior. But this morning, as we were running for our lives, he confronted us and told us that he had been sent to protect us and that if we trust him, he would bring us to safety. And he did just that. He brought us to you."

"I saw no one bring you to me this morning." The Holy Father said. "Our Lord showed me through prayer that you both were to leave Rome with me. We waited for only a minute or two and then we saw you both running around the corner and stop only to decide whether you should get into our vehicle. That's when I had my assistant open the side door and motion to you that it was safe to enter."

"But he talked to us and even told us his name."

"Jenny, wait a minute." I said. "When you asked him who it was that sent him to protect us, he said, I can't tell you that."

"What are you trying to say?" Jenny asked.

A big smile came across the Pope's face.

"My dear child, I suspect Angelo was an angel."

"He must have been." I said. "Remember we joked about how he wore the same clothes every day?"

"Right and we literally watched him disappear into that crowd. I thought that looked strange."

"God works in mysterious ways. When you trust in him, he will always be there to help you. You can thank Angelo through prayer. He will hear you." The Pope said with a smile.

"It's just all so amazing." Jenny reflected as she sat back slowly in her chair.

"You will find that God will always amaze you." The Pope said still smiling. "And if I may, I wanted to share something with you before we go our separate ways. You may be surprised to discover that I was given a copy of each of your pamphlets. I found them to be very thorough. I was drawn in particular to this quote from Our Lady of La Salette:

'I call on the Apostles of the Last Days, the faithful disciples of Jesus Christ who have lived in scorn for the world and for themselves, in poverty and in humility, in scorn and in silence, in prayer and in mortification, in chastity and in union with God, in suffering and unknown to the world. It is time they came out and filled the world with light. Go and reveal yourselves to be my cherished children. I am at your side and within you, provided that your faith is the light which shines upon you in these unhappy days. May your zeal make you famished for the glory and the honor of Jesus Christ. Fight, children of light, you, the few who can see. For now is the time of all times, the end of all ends.'

Pope Benedict leaned in, grasped our hands and looked intently into our eyes.

"You my children are Apostles of the Last Days and leaders in God's remnant army. Our Lady is speaking directly to you. Go out and fill the world with light! She will be at your side. You are among the few who can see. You must multiply your numbers and fight! Have no fear. Trust in Our Lord and he will guide you. This is the time of all times! This is the end of all ends!"

The Holy Father then extended us his blessing and for the short remainder of the flight we sat quietly, absorbing all that he had said. There is nothing so inspiring as to have the Vicar of Christ look directly into your eyes and give a directive with such encouragement. It filled us with such firmness of purpose that we found it impossible to respond.

Within 15 minutes we were on the ground in Lisbon. We said our final goodbyes knowing that this would be the last time we would be in the presence of our Holy Father. It was very emotional. His final words to us were, "Go wake a nation and a world in slumber."

Three hours later Jenny and I were on a plane back to the United States. In our down time we were able to reach out to our parents and to Father Ramos, informing them that we were safe and on our way home. It certainly was a relief to be heading home but we couldn't help but wonder what would become of Italy and of Europe. Within the span of three days, the world had changed and we knew that from this moment forward, it would never be the same again.

Looking out the window, gazing down at the earth below, it was as if a dark cloud was descending upon the entire world. With war on the horizon, the False Prophet would soon destroy the Holy Sacrifice of the Mass, create a false Church and give rise to the Antichrist, the son of perdition, the man of iniquity, the beast. He will rise to power seemingly from out of nowhere disguising himself as a man of peace. He will capture the world's attention and adulation as he takes control of a one world government, one world economy, one world currency and one world religion. Most will succumb to his charm being unschooled in Bible prophecy and the world will be brought to its knees. The Apostles of the last days, God's remnant army, will gallantly fight back, will hold fast to the true faith and will not be defeated. But among their ranks many will be martyred. And in the midst of it all, God will once again give the world the greatest demonstrations of his infinite love. His Hand of Mercy will be extended as The Warning and The Great Miracle serve to bring people back to their senses before it's too late; before His Hand of Justice is forced to fall in a worldwide chastisement that will pave the way for the return of Jesus.

The world must be told! The world must prepare!

End Notes

1. http://the-american-catholic.com/2010/01/24/pope-leo-and-saint-michael-the-archangel/, The American Catholic, Pope Leo and Saint Michael the Archangel, Published Sunday, January 24, A.D. 2010

2. Daniel 12:1

3. https://www.ewtn.com/fatima/apparitions/October.htm, Apparition of 13 October 1917, Eyewitness accounts of The Miracle of the Sun

4. 1 Kings 2:11

5. Jonah 1:17

6. Exodus 10:21-23

7. 1 Kings 18:19-39

8. 1 Kings 17:17-24

9. 1 Chronicles 21:1-14

10. Daniel 6:11

11. Luke 1:56

12. Matthew 2:1-12

13. Luke 2:41-52

14. Luke 3:23

15. Matthew 26:26-30

16. Matthew 26:36-46

17. Luke 22:54-62

18. http://www.ewtn.com/vexperts/showmessage.asp?number=353203 &Pg=&Pgnu=&recnu=

19. Luke 23:33

20. http://www.ewtn.com/vexperts/showmessage.asp?number=586810 &Pg=&Pgnu=&recnu=

21. John 19:19-20

22. Matthew 27:45-50

23. http://www.ewtn.com/vexperts/showmessage.asp?number=308289 &Pg=&Pgnu=&recnu=

24. Luke 24:1-8

25. Acts 9:9

26. 2 Corinthians 11:25

27. Galatians 1:17-18

28. 2 Corinthians 12:7-9

29. Revelation 12:1

30. Matthew 10:16

31. Fatima in Lucia's Own Words, 16th edition, July 2007, 123

32. Ibid., 179

33. Ibid., 123-124

34. "Aurora borealis glows in widest area since 1709" – [Chicago Daily Tribune, January 26, 1938, p.2]

35. Fatima in Lucia's Own Words, 16th edition, July 2007, 197-198

36. Ibid.

37. http://www.fatima.org/essentials/facts/rianjo.asp, The Apparition at Rianjo (1931)

38. http://www.fatima.org/essentials/facts/bishapprov.asp, Approval by the Bishop (1930)

39. https://www.ewtn.com/expert/answers/FatimaConsecration.htm, Fatima Consecration – Chronology, History of the Consecration and Related Events

40. http://www.fatima.org/essentials/opposed/cvrup4.asp, Unsatisfactory Consecrations

41. Ibid.

42. http://www.fatima.org/essentials/opposed/cvrup4.asp, Another Inadequate Consecration

43. http://www.fatima.org/pdf/losservatore/article_8.pdf, Why the Confusion?

44. Ibid.

45. To The Priests Our Lady's Beloved Sons, 18th English Edition, "I Ask for the Consecration of All", March 25, 1984

46. Ibid.

47. http://www.remnantnewspaper.com/Archives/2013-0228-siscoe-bishop-dressed-in-white.htm, A Bishop Dressed in White?

48. Ibid.

49. My interpretation.

50. http://www.fatima.org/essentials/facts/secret.asp, The Third Secret of Fatima

51. http://www.fatima.org/f4b/complete_fatima_timeline.pdf, The Complete Fatima Timeline

52. http://www.fatima.org/thirdsecret/ratzinger.asp, Published Testimony: (November 1984)Cardinal Ratzinger

53. http://www.fatima.org/f4b/complete_fatima_timeline.pdf, The Complete Fatima Timeline

54. Fatima in Lucia's Own Words, 16th edition, July 2007, 215

55. http://www.fatima.org/f4b/complete_fatima_timeline.pdf, The Complete Fatima Timeline

56. Karol Cardinal Wojtyla, "Notable & Quotable," – [Wall Street Journal, November 9, 1978, p.30]

57. http://www.fatima.org/f4b/complete_fatima_timeline.pdf, The Complete Fatima Timeline

58. Diary of Saint Maria Faustina Kowalska - Divine Mercy in My Soul, 950

59. To The Priests Our Lady's Beloved Sons, 18th English Edition

60. My interpretation

61. Ibid.

62. http://www.garabandal.org/story.shtml, The Garabandal Story

63. To The Priests Our Lady's Beloved Sons, 18th English Edition

64. Diary of Saint Maria Faustina Kowalska - Divine Mercy in My Soul, 83

65. http://www.thepopeinred.com/secret.htm, Apparition of the Blessed Virgin on the Mountain of La Salette the 19th of September, 1846

66. Ibid.

67. To The Priests Our Lady's Beloved Sons, 18th English Edition

68. http://www.thepopeinred.com/secret.htm, Apparition of the Blessed Virgin on the Mountain of La Salette the 19th of September, 1846

69. Ibid.

70. Ibid.

71. http://www.sspxasia.com/Newsletters/2003/Jul-Dec/Secret_of_La_Salette.htm, Discovery of the Secret of La Salette

72. https://www.youtube.com/watch?v=IkebbEAAqWA, Twin Crusade – Burma, documentary, ABC Australia, 2000

73. http://content.time.com/time/world/article/0,8599,2054474,00.html, The Twin Terrors, Time Magazine, Feb 7, 2000

74. http://www.nytimes.com/2013/11/03/world/asia/briefly-myan-mars-gods-army-twins-reunite.html?_r=0, Briefly, Myanmar's 'God's Army' Twins Reunite, AP, Nov 2, 2013

75. http://www.bbc.com/news/technology-31042477, Office puts chips under staff's skin

76. http://www.theguardian.com/g2/story/0,3604,347432,00.html Two Little Boys, The Guardian, Jul 27, 2000

77. To The Priests Our Lady's Beloved Sons, 18th English Edition

78. http://www.newadvent.org/cathen/09771a.htm, Catholic Encyclopedia, Masonry (Freemasonry)

79. Ibid.

80. Ibid.

81. Pope Leo XIII, Humanum Genus, paragraph 31.

82. http://www.salvemariaregina.info/SalveMariaRegina/SMR-155/ Our%20Lady%20of%20Good%20Success.html, Our Lady of Good Success

83. Pope Benedict XVI, A Turning Point for Europe?, Second Edition, 45.

⬖ Chapter Three

Redefinition of Labour

One of the ways of attacking the myths of fear and pain in childbirth is to redefine labour. Labour is usually broken down into three stages. The first stage begins with regular uterine contractions. For our purposes we should divide labour into four stages, and include the preliminary stage of labour. The preliminary stage of labour ideally begins three months prior to conception when the mother and her partner begin to prepare themselves physically, mentally, and spiritually for pregnancy. It is during this preliminary stage that all the preparations for true labour should begin. It is here that the prevention of maternal and foetal distress and paternal isolation begins. Buying into the negative myths of childbirth affect the regulation of a mother's hormones in a negative way, which then signal to an overflow which, in turn, leads to imbalance in the autonomic nervous system and the brain of the foetus.

By the second trimester, the psychological impressions of the autonomic nervous system are now able to be sensated by the higher brain centers. Thus, it is important to remember that your baby is under the same stress you are experiencing. This is a most important awareness for the fathers, as well. It would serve you well, dads, to attempt to provide the most serene atmosphere possible. The behavior of the father, which oftentimes becomes erratic during pregnancy, has a great influence upon the mother's feelings and behavior, and thus on the baby.

How many times can an unborn child endure stressful emotions before it affects her/his personality structure. The ability of the family dynamic to directly influence the foetus should be taken into consideration so that the pregnancy can be a time of maternal/

paternal/foetal bonding. Many feelings arise spontaneously during pregnancy, and thus can't be dealt with prior to their emergence. However, when they do arise it is important that they be dealt with rather than denied. It has been my observation that the mother is willing to deal with most of the conflicts of pregnancy and motherhood. However, oftentimes she does not get support from the father. He frequently seems frightened of facing even the slightest feelings and fears that emerge. He therefore withdraws, which triggers the mother's fear of abandonment. The father's withdrawal is often triggered by his own fear of abandonment. Now we have a vicious cycle — each afraid of being abandoned, and each experiencing their greatest fear. What must the innocent ego of the foetus be experiencing across the neuro-hormonal pathway? How can this be resolved so all needs are met? The solution is simple, yet not so very easy.

It is important to be who we are. It is important to articulate the myriad of feelings that arise as a result of pregnancy. You are not alone in these feelings. You are alone when you don't speak of them, when you isolate yourself and distance yourself from your mate. There is an appropriateness to taking a retreat during pregnancy. However, this should not be done in a hostile way, but in a self-searching, loving way. It is proper and fitting for the father to go off by himself in nature for three days or so, and for the mother to do the same —a time for a vision quest of sorts, a time to get in touch with one's own spirit and life force and true inner desires and needs. When we are quiet it is easier to know what we really want and need. When we really know what we want and need, we can more readily ask directly for it or give it to ourselves. When we meet our own needs it is then easier to meet the needs of our partner and of our children. All of these emotions, thoughts, and feelings affect the onset and outcome of true labor. Thus, you can see the importance of the preparatory stage. This perhaps is the most important stage of all.

The preparatory stage of labor is a time of listening — listening to your own inner voices, to the voices of your partner, and to the messages of your baby. The baby's main path of communication is through kicking. The baby often kicks when the mother moves from one position to another. He stops kicking when he/she is again comfortable. Loud noises can also stimulate a baby to kick vehemently, as can foetal distress. Extreme negative emotions felt by the mother can also create an uncomfortable environment for the baby, which he manifests by kicking.

Exercise:

1. Write out all your reasons for wanting a child, and be as honest with yourself as you can. Write all your reasons for wanting a girl child. Write all your reasons for wanting a boy child.

2. Now separate all the reasons for having a child — boy or girl — that fall under the category of persona (i.e., the personality that you want to present to the world).

3. What is your purpose in life?

4. How will having a child enhance your purpose in life?

After you and your support person have done this exercise, read it aloud to someone of the same sex and discuss it, and then read it aloud to each other and discuss it.

Now let us take a look at some of the pictures people have drawn in the birthing classes to illustrate their emotions, along with their explanations, so you can see that you are not alone in your myriad of feelings.

Corinne's Explanation of Her Picture: I divide the page in half, negative side and positive side. Baby Maureen is supposed to be sucking her thumb. I think she looks like Jonathan (father), and it turns out her thumb ends up looking like his moustache.

We've been only two for so long that I really wonder what it will be like to be three. I'm not really afraid...perhaps a little; more curious than anything. What will happen to our romance? Will it disappear? How much time will we have for loving each other?

That's me reading a baby care book. I'm beginning to realize there is so much that I don't know, so much that I didn't know. I just found out how to fold a diaper.

This is a savings and a checking account. Shortly I'll be losing one of my clients, which on the one hand is fine, as I'll have some time, but on the other hand it takes out a big chunk of my income. How will I create this much more income while caring for Maureen?

And then there are two of me. I actually don't know how many of me there will need to be to do all that has to be done.

On the positive side: There's a part of me that is afraid of not being selfless enough. Then I realize that the selflessness could also lead me to do things which I think might be fun, like the zoo, and yet the zoo is certainly not something I would do or we would do if we didn't have a baby. We also love to travel, both for pleasure and our work. I realize I drew two African animals. Africa could be a fun trip to take with the baby.

One of the nice things will be looking at the world through new eyes. That will be the most fun. I haven't been to Disneyland since I was little. It would be a fun place to go with a child who thinks Mickey Mouse is real.

The last picture is of us on a Sunday night cocooning before it was popular. I'm nursing Maureen and she fits easily into our already cozy scene.

Jonathan's Picture: I see myself as a link between Corinne and Maureen. I see Maureen as a heart surrounded by a white light. I see us all as centered on the ground and a rainbow over us.

Joyce's Drawings (she did two): The first drawing cleared the way for the second. In drawing #1, Joyce is grasping the tree for support. In the right-hand corner is her career as a litigation attorney, the persona of whom she does not like. On top we see the world circumscribed by the same color as her masculine work world. Joyce expresses that there is an entire world out there, and "because of time restrictions I may not be able to experience all I want."

"In the left-hand corner is a much-loved godchild and the conflict in seeing the dark side of the child's parent. That scene brings me much pleasure and great pain. On the left is the garden that gives my life solace and creative expression."

Picture #2 is the way she wants it all to be. "Here I feel safe, serene and free of all ambivalence except that my engagement ring is gone because it no longer fits on my finger. Will I ever be able to have that symbol of freedom and romance, and the maiden back again, or do I now only wear my wedding band? The healing white light flows throughout my body, keeping me well and safe." (The white light is an image we use in every class, an image of our connection to the omniscience of the universe and the healing power of nature.)

Christopher's Picture: He, too, loves the solace of gardening and their garden; thus, he placed them both there. (It was also easier to draw flowers than legs and feet, he confessed.)

His shoulders are broad and he is willing to be as much support as necessary. The white light also shines down upon the baby, keeping her in the proper position for birthing, and ready to begin to aid in the passage through the birth canal.

These two fathers are not necessarily the norm. They are how many of the fathers portray themselves or would like to portray themselves. However, toward the end of the last trimester many of the fathers become more willing to face their fears. It is also part of our culture that the husband is to have symbolically large shoulders, when in fact that role may be one of considerable anxiety to him, at least in some situations.

This picture depicts this father as very supportive. This is, in fact, how he wished to be. He was, in reality, very frightened of losing his wife as a playmate, friend and lover. He was also afraid that he would faint during transition. Thus, he gave himself permission to leave at that time if he became frightened. As it turned out, he in fact witnessed the entire labour and birthing process. When he became anxious, he sat in a chair and observed quietly and in awe.

The drawing and discussion of these pictures inevitably brings up the mother's and father's new role. The mother, feeling initially comfortable thinking about decorating the nursery, buying baby clothes, getting all in order, is confronted by the father, who is beginning to feel left out and isolated. The mother continues to fantasize about holding her baby and caring for it; in many cases, thoughts about suckling are very soothing and comforting. Oftentimes the father's fantasy is — when can we make love again, when can we have a weekend away? After birthing, and for the first few weeks, the mother becomes more obsessed with the baby, and oftentimes doesn't want to even leave the house and hearth. The father hasn't gained a child, but rather he's lost his lover, his playmate, his nurturer and friend to this demanding little suckling creature. It is to these fears that the fathers must speak.

Exercise:
Mother and Father:
1. Make a list of fears you had as a child that you still have today.
2. Make a list of fears that you had as an adolescent that you still have today.
3. Make a list of pre-pregnancy adult fears.
4. Make a list of fears that have come into being since pregnancy began.
5. Make a list of the fears that you are aware of that your mother and father either manifested or talked about.
6. Make a list of the fears you experience your partner as having.

Decide what fears you are willing to live with and what fears you want to discard. Now make a decision to do whatever work is necessary to eliminate, to diminish, or to accept certain fears in your life. Decide what fears you definitely don't want to pass on to your child. Even if we try to hide our fears and deny them to ourselves, we cannot hide them from our children.

One of the fathers told a story of his mother's relationship to her first child, his older brother. He said that she was riddled with fears which incapacitated her to the point of being unable to leave the house shortly after the baby's birth. The mother's fears escalated and culminated in the baby's having a perforated ulcer at six months of age.

It is important to recognize when we need professional help and to reach out for it. There need be no shame; we are all fallible human beings doing the best that we can do alone. Why not decide to do the best that we can do with some help if we need it. We deserve support. We are all interdependent on each other as in nature. We truly can learn a lot from the birds and the bees.

LABOUR — FIRST STAGE

If at any time during the first stage of labour you feel stressed, your brain waves will be altered, your endorphins will be depleted, and the production of catecholamines will be stimulated, which will, in turn, block the remaining endorphins. Thus you will feel an increase in pain. It is most important, therefore, that your support person take charge and create and maintain a relaxed and stress-free environment in which you can labour. It is your support person who can deal with the hospital staff, so that you can remain in harmony with the work your body is doing, so that you and your body are one.

The family bonding begins while the child is in utero, and of course continues throughout the child's life, primarily during the first twelve years. The bonding that is established between the relaxed mother and father during labour, birthing and post-partum is ever so important. It is here in the midst of this tender loving care among the three that the foundation for the healthy family is established.

The purpose of the first stage of labour is to fully open the cervix. This is done through the contraction of the uterine muscles. The longitudinal muscles that run from the bottom of the uterus fundus begin to contract. As long as the mother remains relaxed during and between these first-stage contractions, these longitudinal muscles relax. The circular muscles retract, which pull the cervix up over the baby's head. Together they work to flatten and efface the cervix. As long as the mother remains relaxed, the cervix begins to dilate, and the uterus is able to do its first stage expulsive activity without contradiction (that is, the expulsive message does not meet with resistance, the mother keeps her jaw relaxed, her lips apart, her rectal sphincter relaxed, her entire perineal area relaxed). In this way the constrictor nerve muscles remain inactive, and all muscles and nerves work together toward expulsion. Relaxation also helps to maintain an active blood supply to the uterus and helps to eliminate the waste products of the muscles' actions.

By the end of the first stage, the cervix is fully dilated. It is important to remember at this stage that your mind/body in harmony knows exactly how to birth your baby. Let us not, at this moment, make a bifurcation of mind/body. It is when you're apart from your mind/body connection that the following occurs.

DISHARMONY
Mind = Thoughts = Neurotransmitters

Will I bleed too much?
Will my lip open?
Will I do it the right way?
Will the baby be all right?
I am too tired to do this.
Will my support person be supportive?
Will I remember every thing from my classes?
I am scared.
Will this hurt?
Will I die?

MIND

Will the baby be born alive?

Will I like the baby?

Will my support person like the baby?

Will I be fat?

Will I ever lose all the weight I gained?

Will I ever feel sexual again?

Will I still be sexually attractive to my partner?

DISHARMONY
Negative emotions - Neurotransmitter - Bodily reactions

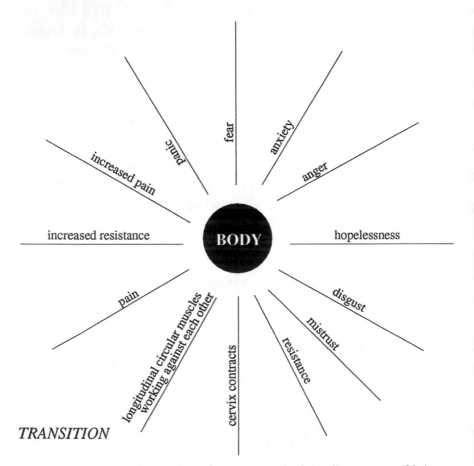

TRANSITION

Transition is the time from the end of the first stage of labour to the beginning of the second. This is the most difficult and the briefest period of labour. It is at this time (when you are about 7-8 centimeters dilated) that you will need the most support and encouragement and reassurance.

The feelings during this stage are myriad. It is my suspicion that they come at this time due to our natural fear of being totally open. We all have defense mechanisms that safely protect us from ourselves and our world. Each human being needs a certain amount of denial. At this stage our physical body doesn't comply with this need.

Instead, it defies this survival mechanism by stretching us to our limits. Thus, we become frightened and irritable and anxious, a bit disoriented and exhausted. This is only temporary.

Support person, stay close at hand. Be encouraging. Allow her to be dependent on you at this stage. Honor this physiological discomfort with more attention and comforting reassurance.

At transition, you are about to fulfill your potential, i.e., you are going to let all that is within the birth canal out. Whenever we fulfill our potential, we have a wonderful feeling of nearing completion, but this abandonment of ego to spirit also can feel like a sense of loss, maybe even a feeling of approaching death; for in some ways we have been taught that when we are complete, we shall die. Therefore, the feeling of "I can have it all" can be a frightening thing. Your limits are expanding. This glimpse of the marvelous possibilities that are available in life is one of the reasons for the great anxiety some women experience during the dilation from seven to ten centimeters.

If the door to your unconscious is open, you can most certainly be assured of an easy transition.

Through the practice and understanding of all the exercises, including third trimester dream analysis, you can experience your contractions and final dilation of your cervix with a feeling of excitement rather than fear.

Exercises for Eliminating Distress

Your goal is to empty your mind of all thoughts by concentrating on your third eye, which is explained in the chapter on hypnosis. If any thoughts do enter your mind, take immediate control of them by repeating to yourself, "Relax my jaw, focus on my exhalation, breathe all the way through my body. That's it! Now keep my jaw relaxed, breathe all the way through my body, allow my exhalation to be complete." Keep repeating this as a mantra.

Taking all of this into consideration, you can now see the advantage of letting your thoughtful mind take a lovely, long rest in a garden somewhere while you connect to your intuitive mind. Let go of your left brain. It is overdressed for the occasion and out of place here. Next time you make love, convert to your rational mind, and see how easy it is to relax and to have an orgasm. It will be next to impossible. You might even find yourself having dyspareunia (painful intercourse).

Imagine a high wire act criticizing herself as she walks tremulously above the crowd. "My foot is going to slip. I'll never make it to the other side." A bit ridiculous, no?

Have you ever played golf or tennis? Next time you play, don't keep your eye on the ball; criticize your serve, connect to your observing ego and your critical faculties. You might find yourself having tennis elbow or bursitis of your shoulder.

When you ride a trotting horse, imagine yourself sitting the trot comfortably, rolling with the gait of the horse. Now imagine yourself posting the trot, being gently tossed into the air by the movement of the horse. All is well. Now resist the movement and you bounce all over, out of control. You want the horse to stop, so you squeeze your legs in fear. The horse receives this message and, being well trained, he recognizes it as a signal to go. He takes off into a canter. You resist even more. You pull back on the reins and squeeze with your legs. Now you are telling the horse to stop with your hands, and you are telling him to go with your legs. Not only are you out of balance, but you manage to get a confused horse who is doing his best to follow the rules of the creature on his back, this creature who seems to think she knows how to get him to move. Now everyone is out of balance, and you end up on the ground in a rather uncomfortable position.

Get back up on the horse and pay attention at the walk (the preparatory first stage of labour). Let the horse be the body and you the intuitive mind. Now close your eyes for a moment and imagine yourself feeling the rhythm of the horse and looking in the direction you want to go. You move together; now you flow as one. Allow yourself to be in rhythm with your body during transition. It can be as easy or as difficult as riding a horse.

SECOND STAGE OF LABOUR

The purpose of this stage is to push the baby out. Once the cervix is fully dilated, you will begin to push during the contractions. In between, you will feel very relaxed. You might even doze off, only to awaken feeling energized and exhilarated, ready to work hard to move toward your goal of pushing your baby out into the world. With your mouth slightly opened and jaw relaxed, your body in a good position for you to push, with no resistance from your rectum, your vaginal walls, or your perineal muscles, you push the baby lower and lower into your vagina. Finally the crowning of your little princess or prince occurs, i.e., the very top of the baby's head is continuously visible at the vagina. Your doctor or midwife now gently guides your baby's head as it is emerging. Now it is most important for you to relax when you feel a stretching. Breathe all the way out through your perineal floor. Soon the baby's head will cause a natural anesthetic effect. Continue to relax.

THIRD STAGE OF LABOUR

This is the expulsion of the placenta, which naturally occurs usually within one-half hour after the birth. Nursing your baby immediately after birth releases hormones into your system that cause your uterus to contract, thus aiding the expulsion of the placenta with little or no bleeding.

Not power but pairing, not dominance but sharing. When a man connects to his nurturing instinct paired with his spouse, he is able to celebrate the fact that new life emerges from a woman's body.

Men became farmers in order to bring life to earth. This is no longer honored by our advancing technological society. Men have tried to expand and cross-fertilize through technology. Some have done this so aggressively that they have created a movement towards our annihilation. The choices we make in our daily lives are crucial and remarkable. Men have a tremendous ability to contribute to our cultural growth. Through an active participation in the birthing process, men can move away from their responses and stone walls of fear, and can begin to walk calmly in the peaceful postures of their character.

I was speaking with a father who had just observed his first birth, although it was his fourth child. He said he was profoundly affected. He did not participate with his spouse, as he was afraid he would faint. It was all he could do to be there. He did not faint, however. He watched in awe the great miracle. He is a pornography star and told me that he found it difficult to "perform" in his next two films, as he began to view in a different light the sexual activity for which he was paid to engage. He had connected to his participating power rather than to his dominating power.

The birthing opened his canal of responsible, loving care, as opposed to his oppressive sexual dominance channels. He could not "rise to the occasion", according to his terminology.

He had been humbled. His manly pride no longed rested in the dominance of his erection. He was beginning to realize a greater power — that of transformation and birth, of participation and responsibility.

I ask you now on a scale of one to ten (ten being the greatest degree of fear and pain) how frightened are you of birthing and how much pain do you think you have to endure?

Most of the mothers I have asked score around a seven on both questions. By the time they have dealt with the issues at the end of the class, the birthing score is a three. Decide now on a realistic goal for yourself. If you want to be a three, make this decision, and also make a commitment to do whatever it takes to get you to the beneficial way of thinking that will bring you to a three.

❖ Chapter Four

The Path to Universal Truth That Lies Within Each One of Us

In order to be fulfilled, we need to know what our nature is, to reconnect to that nature, and to finally strive toward achieving the full potential of our self. The conflict is always: Shall I be true to my nature or to the culture that is imposed upon me, and how shall I know the difference?

Through your dreams you can connect your instinct with your life's plan. You no longer have to be beholden to the patriarchy or to your parents. You can become integrated; you can supply your own ideals and goals to the birthing process as well as to other areas of your life. It is through your emotional association to your dream content that the message of the dream is uncovered. It is the analyst's job to play back to you your emotionally charged associations. The dreamer is the architect and the soil. The dream is the blueprint. The analyst is merely the contractor who provides the proper grading of the land, so that the building can safely take place, and can be coordinated into a coherent whole. Or, if you'd like to go Hollywood, the dreamer is the writer, the instinct the director, the soul does the lighting and the photography, and the analyst joins the dreamer as co-producer, taking all the raw material and continuing it to fruition.

We can even program ourselves to dream. I was working at a week-long cancer retreat with a young woman who had breast cancer. She had been very prominent in her own business, which fulfilled both her need for autonomy and for creativity. She gave this business up totally in order to become a mother. She much enjoyed her children, and had a very good relationship with her husband. She decided that she wanted to live, but in order to do so, she knew that she would have to reconnect to her creativity. She felt a bit tormented by this thought, as she had no idea what she wanted to do. Her husband had just opened a paint supply store for Julie, so she could get out of the house. Julie said it did fill her time, but she didn't know if it was what she really wanted to do.

I told her that an easy way to find out what she really wants is to tell herself that she would like to receive an answer in a dream. I told her that she would probably have this dream by the end of the week, and we could do a dream session at that time.

We always have a three-hour lunch break, so that patients and staff can rest, meditate, exercise, and/or do their assignments for the afternoon session. After one of these breaks, Julie had a big smile on her face and her whole being seemed happy. "I took a nap," she said, "and I had the dream. I know exactly what I want to do. I don't want any part of the store. I talked with James, and he agreed that we would close it ASAP. I used to paint, and I am going to set aside time each week to do that, and believe it or not, I am going to take ballet lessons. It's something I always thought about, but was afraid of."

There was a new freedom about Julie for the rest of the week. She had allowed her life force to take over, and it showed.

The more spiritual we become, the more aware we become. The more ego-involved we become, the less conscious we become, and the instinct's ability to emerge fulfilled in consciousness diminishes.

Much of our consciousness is at the raw, instinctive level. Along comes the world of time, minutes, days, each a new experience, maybe some very similar to the ones before. Through these experiences an ever-changing ego state is imposed upon us; thus, our ego becomes conscious of what our society is conscious of. This, however, is not our true consciousness. Our true consciousness is repressed. We begin to act as if we and the world's perception of us are one and the same. It is through the intensity of our emotions that our true consciousness is kept alive. Our emotions are an expression of an ego's imposition upon us. There does come a time when we can let go of the vehemence of these emotions, and that is when we engage the spirit, when we engage our own omniscient "self" to act as a mediator between our reality and our external world's reality. Of course, this is not static. Daily, we must engage our spirit to reconcile with the demons of the ego.

Our instincts are the seeds of truth, our ego the unpredictable weather, and our spirit the great Rain and Sun God who tells us what we must do behaviourally to survive and to flourish. After much ado, we finally recognize our own reality, realizing that some seeds do well in sand, some high in the mountains, some on the vast plains, some by the breeze of the sea, and some in the sensuous rain forest. Feeling and expressing the raging emotions of trial and error are paths toward the quietude of knowing the spirit. We must listen or we shall remain tortured. Once we have arrived at this place, we can BE. Here we are not possessed by thought, by feeling, by ego, by undeveloped instinct; here we have arrived at freedom. Here we are a perfect trinity of ego-instinct-soul.

It is through this process, through the associations to the dream fragments, and through the interpretation of dreams, especially those of the last trimester, that you are freed to give yourself full permission to birth your baby in a conscious, joyous manner.

If we look at illness in general, and pain and complications in childbirth, as a function of physiological, psychological, and social influences, then we need to examine the thread that links them. It has been said that structure is adapted to function. When we see the order in the universe, we can easily accept the logic of the structure and function of the body. Specifically, let us focus on the uterus, as that is the organ of interest here and now. The uterus has been demonstrated to have pain receptors that register excessive tension and/or laceration of the tissues. These pain receptors are TENSION and LACERATION specific and respond to no other pain stimuli. The purpose of pain is to benefit the body, not to harm it. It is a protective mechanism used to inform the body. From this information, an interpretation of the message is then made, and we either defend against the danger or prevent the impending danger from happening.

Childbirth is a normal and natural function. Pain is not a normal occurrence in a healthy organ. During childbirth, the circular muscle fibers of the uterus relax to allow dilation of the cervix. At the same time, the longitudinal muscle fibers contract to further push the child down through the passage. It is important to know that the body is able to regulate the sensation of pain. Our body has a class of biochemicals called endorphins (internal morphine) which act as the body's own natural painkiller. Since our preconception of childbirth is one of pain, and since the neurochemical makeup of our body is such that it can mirror any mental event, it would be advantageous to alter our thinking, thus altering the network of body and mind information.

Imagine, if you will, a day at the beach. The water is calm. There isn't a swell in sight. There's a gentle breeze. The sun is at its zenith. The water feels cool and delightful, and you have not a care in the world. You decide to rent a raft and to float and to dream. You feel marvelous. You're totally relaxed and content. All of a sudden, you see people rushing from the water onto the beach, and you hear the lifeguard shouting through his megaphone, "Everyone out of the water — SHARKS!!" How would you feel? What would you do? You would probably feel terrified and rush from the water as quickly as possible.

Now, what is it that caused your fear? It was not the shark, as you didn't even see it. What caused your fear was your belief in the lifeguard's words and your own belief system about sharks. However, our body doesn't know that it is reacting to our belief system and not to an actual shark. The fear creates a chemical pathway that sends a message from our brain to our body. Thus, our mind has projected itself into our body, causing our body to react or interact.

In labour, when the pain receptors are stimulated, it means that our body is getting a message to relax. The uterus is experiencing excessive tension. The tension causes the circular muscle fibers to contract, thus resisting the work of the longitudinal muscles. Therefore, the uterus is working against itself.

To prevent your body from running away with you, the necessary engaging and calming of the mind/body needs to be initiated long before labour has begun. The prevention of the stimulus of the pain receptors should have begun at twenty weeks through the weekly practice of the hypnotic techniques. Let us use Christina as an example of early engagement.

Christina had been attending the Leclaire hypnosis and childbirth classes with her husband, Thomas. They were both enjoying the classes, and felt very excited about having their second child using hypnosis. During Christina's twenty-fifth week, her father was hospitalized for cancer, and her mother spent every waking minute at his side. Christina had many feelings about this, which at that time she did not articulate. At twenty-six weeks Christina went to her obstetrician, and was found to have an outbreak of herpes, her first flare-up in ten years. At twenty-seven weeks her baby had turned to a podalic version. If the herpes flared up and did not disappear, a Cesarean section would be necessary. If the baby did not turn on her own, she would need assistance.

Christina was very aware of the connection between her mind and body, and called for a private appointment. At that time we discussed her feelings about her mother's being unavailable for her. She told me of her first birth, which was attended by both her mother and father, her husband, and her sisters. She was beginning to be concerned that her father might not be well enough to attend the birth, and if he were not, her mother probably would not leave his side for very long. On top of that, her four-year-old was going to be at the birth, and Christina's mom had accepted to be the support person to her granddaughter. Now this, too, would have to change. After talking about her feelings and after drawing a picture of herself and her herpes, we made a hypnotherapy and healing tape. We also discussed that the best way to get to the bottom of this was for Christina to record her dreams. Christina agreed. She also agreed to play her hypnosis tape daily. During that week, Christina had a dream. Following is that dream, as told to me by Christina:

"I was in a movie set on a patio area. Phil Donahue and Marlo Thomas were sitting on a bench beside a low white brick wall. There were small plants in large planters in a room. The set wasn't getting built, and the movie wasn't being made fast enough. All of a sudden, young (in their early twenties) men and woman came out dressed in military uniforms, but they weren't Nazis. They were taking people away. I had to do something — I realized I had no place to hide. Marlo and Phil were separated by a partition, and only their feet could now be seen.

A young man started to take me. I went over to a young woman, who started to frisk me, but didn't finish. I took her arm and told her, "I want to go with my husband, Thomas." He then suddenly appeared. They were going to take him away. I took the woman's arm and went over to Thomas. I was really upset. I had to go with my husband. We went into a dark room like a theater. There was a man in his fifties or sixties crying, and a woman sitting in the shadows. Something bad was going on in the room."

We worked together on Christina's associations and the analysis of the dream over a few sessions. Here is the "essence of the dream" as written by Christina:

"Marlo Thomas and Phil Donahue represented people worthy of making a contribution. Marlo specifically represents someone who does what she wants to do and feels good about her contribution to the world. I have respect for Phil. He also does what he wants and has integrity, and they both represent financial security and success. I could see their feet under the partition. She wore heels and a skirt, and he had brand-new shoes and slacks. Their feet were on the ground, the way I want to feel and be. My father seemed to be the man weeping in the theater, and my mother was sitting in the shadow. I was relating to making some of the same mistakes that he had made. One of the problems is having to be "ill" as he had been. The realization was that I do not want to manifest these problems of "unworthiness." I don't want to blindly follow my husband, as my mother did my father. I could break this pattern by staying conscious instead of walking into the darkness (unconsciousness). I am not my father. I am not my mother.

Through my dream I discovered why I was creating being ill during my pregnancy. Hypnosis and the dream work helped me to control my illness, so I did not have to have a Cesarean section."

One week after the dream analysis, Christina's herpes had disappeared and her baby had turned around, and was again in proper position for birthing. She now felt ready to give birth. Two days after Christina's due date, I received a phone call from Christina. She was in the birthing room and all was going well. We spoke briefly, interrupted by two contractions.

Christina's husband, her four-year-old, and her sister attended the birth. Her mother stopped by for a visit, as her father was now home and doing well. At one point during transition, Christina looked at the crowd and, seeing her family's mounting tension, half in jest and half creating the right environment, the right "set" for herself, she instructed, "Now, one-two-three, everyone take a deep breath and let it go—relax." They all laughed and the tension subsided. Unmedicated and delighted, she birthed a healthy baby girl.

Christina notes, "Hypnosis was a tremendous help to me during my pregnancy and the birth of my daughter. I was able to focus, to relax, and to feel confident. The instruction allowed me to prepare myself for childbirth. I was ready, and I had the techniques to aid my body to do what I naturally know how to do.

"I was not afraid, because I was able to transcend the common belief, a myth, that one must be 'in pain' to give birth. We arrived at the hospital around 1:00 p.m., and I gave birth at 5:18 p.m. Most of that time I walked around. Our daughter's birth was peaceful and satisfying."

Instead of remaining in denial, Christina was willing to free herself. All fears and anxieties that remain subdued in the unconscious work steadily and stealthily on the "involuntary" muscles, the glands and the organs.

Analytic dream work, especially in the last trimester, can facilitate a woman's return to all the wonderful sensations and consciousness of childbirth. It is through the dream that we can effectively unmask and explore the reciprocity of these psychological and social influences. However, receiving and recalling the dream is only a part of the process. We must now engage the active imagination to begin the investigation of the dreamer/dream.

Jung discusses active imagination and differentiates it from fantasy as follows:

"...fantasy is mere nonsense, a phantom, a fleeting impression; but imagination is active, purposeful, creation. A fantasy is more or less your own invention, and remains on the surface of personal things and conscious expectations. But active imagination, as the term denotes, means that the images have a life of their own and that the symbolic events develop according to their own logic — that is, of course, if your conscious reason does not interfere. You begin by concentrating upon a starting point. "

It is here that the analyst can help to set the proper environment. The starting point begins with the actual telling of the dream. A second telling of the dream puts the dreamer into closer contact with the dream state. As the dreamer is describing and telling the content, the analyst is visualizing all the images, thus becoming more in touch with the diaphanous fabric of the dream state.

The attention focused, the atmosphere prepared, the dreamer can now begin her association and active imagination. It is important that she speaks of the characters and the sets in the dream as though they were happening now — the analyst listens, never interrupting the flow, questioning only to uncover more material, talking only to further open the imagination and association. The state of the analyst and the dreamer are on the same "wavelength," so to speak. The analyst becomes the wide-angled lens of the dreamer/dream, aligning with the expansion of the available knowledge.

Let us now look at a few of the most often asked questions regarding dreams and dream work.

1. How can I remember my dreams?

The first step is desire. Ask yourself if you really want to remember your dreams and why. If you decide that you would like to remember them, get yourself into an hypnotic or relaxed state and begin to imagine an inner guide. The guide can take any form, any form at all; there is no right or wrong image or sensation. If you have difficulty seeing or sensing an inner guide, create one that you would like to have. One of my guides is my grandmother who is now dead. I have seen a dove, my grandfather, a great-grandmother whom I never met, the Virgin Mary, a deer, and a group of rabbits who led me to an old Mexican woman whom I met ten years ago (and never thought of again until she emerged as a guide). When you have a guide, speak to it and let it know that you would very much like to remember your dreams tonight; that you look forward to falling asleep and to dreaming, and that you trust your guide will aid you in the recall of your dreams.

When you awaken in the morning, before you open your eyes or move about in bed, become aware of how you feel and then ask yourself, "What did I dream?" Stay in the awakening position during the retrieval of the dream. Dreams require attention and respect in order to be remembered. It is also advantageous to trust that you will remember at least a piece of a dream the first night that you try. Focus your attention on the area between your two eyebrows, also called your third eye. Relax into it and allow the dream fragments to come into play. They may at first announce themselves as bits and pieces of a puzzle, and shortly you will be able to frame them together into a whole. With your eyes barely open, reach for the pen and paper you're keeping at hand and write down the dream. Further recall often occurs while you are writing. Another important aspect of recall is allowing yourself full rein of exploration without judgement of the seemingly most absurd, incoherent or obvious dream. Even a mere fragment of a dream can trigger significant associations, understandings and changes. It is best to approach any dream with a childlike wonder and curiosity.

2. Can I interpret my own dreams, or do I need an analyst?

An analyst is certainly beneficial. However, it is your dream. One of the best ways of interpreting the dream on your own is to take the most confusing aspect of it, and begin to write down anything that comes into your head — free associate, stream of consciousness thoughts will flow — and write automatically without judgment or editing. The process may seem as absurd as the dream. Allow yourself complete freedom without censorship. It is as though the pen had a life of its own. Just write as rapidly as you can, the first thing that enters your mind.

This works for most people. However, Dawn (thirty-seven weeks pregnant), a sculptor, had a great deal of difficulty expressing herself through painting, drawing, or writing (two-dimensional). She received great benefit from the dreams only after we worked on it together in the group atmosphere. She was having trouble associating to the dream content, so each person read Dawn's dream aloud to her. With each reading of the dream, Dawn opened up a bit more. Here is the dream and some of Dawn's feelings about it (Dawn knew that she was having a boy):

"Last night I dreamt about holding our baby in my arms. She cuddled up to me for awhile until she opened her eyes. They were the most beautiful grey eyes. We looked into each other's eyes with moments of ecstasy and love; then her beautiful eyes grew larger and opened wider and she arched her back, trying to get away from me. Suddenly, she was about two-and-a-half to three years old and wanted to be fed a bottle by her father. I felt so rejected by her hatred for me, which seemed to come out often. I chased her around the room closing doors. She crawled under the chair shrieking when I grabbed her legs."

After much work on the dream, both privately and in group, these are Dawn's final comments:

"It was like looking into my own eyes as an infant and being both the mother and the infant at the same time. Emotionally I was feeling both the mother's feelings and the infant's feelings simultaneously. The furniture in the room, specifically my paternal grandmother's chair, holds a memory of a day when my dad was real sick and he sat in the chair all night. When I was little, between ages (four and eight), I was afraid that monsters were trying to pull me under my bed. I had a secret ritual that made me safe. I would put my legs out of bed, touch the chair and then touch my dad, and I would feel safe. When the mother in the dreams kept closing doors, it reminded me of a room I had as an adolescent; in that house I had my own private exit. I felt comfortable in that room. I have a hard time being in a room if the doors and windows are shut.

Then I began to feel sad and deprived of a nurturer. Then I remembered Rose, a woman whom my parents employed to help with the housekeeping and to care for me part-time. (As Dawn recalled all of this, she was dressed in a wonderfully frivolous dress, covered with roses.) Rose worked hard all day and then at night she would visit the sick in the hospital. She was involved in her church and was religious."

As Dawn first spoke of Rose, she began to cry. She realized her love for this woman and how much she missed her.

"I had forgotten her," she said, weeping. "I feel I have been given a gift. The feelings of the rejection of the mother didn't feel so scary. I didn't feel so guilty. The other women shared their feelings about their mothers. They could all understand that the baby was afraid that her mother couldn't nourish her. I realized that it wasn't such a horrible reaction. It was understandable. I had been feeling guilty that I had been rejecting my mother and that I caused her pain. The other women being so accepting made me feel less guilty. I feel more whole now. Yes, I did get nurtured from Rose and my father and my mother, and I now feel confident that I can break that pattern of several generations of women in our family not being nurtured.

I have already begun to change by allowing me to nurture myself by doing things that I want to do and by taking care of my own hunger instead of being so dependent on my husband.

After the dream work I had an enjoyable visit with my mother. It was different from other visits. She seemed calmer. I felt like she wasn't reacting to things that I was saying like she was feeling rejected. She talked to me about herself and one of her friends, and that was interesting to me.

I also decided to do a ritual out in nature — a doll was involved, a doll that came from Peru and was dressed in a Pre-Columbian fabric. She had the weird energy of an ancient object taken in the wrong way from a burial ground. I wanted to heal this energy with my feminine energy."

3. If I interpret the dream myself, how can I be assured of knowing that I haven't fooled myself?

When we awaken from a dream, there is a mist that rests somewhere within us. It is a bit unsettling. We are not certain of where it lies or what it asks of us. It is like a kitten having a ball of fur that it must release, like a bride having a veil in front of her eyes which, when lifted, enables her to see her beloved clearly. Each dream has an emotional component to it. It is this emotion that is misted in the night; it is this emotion that must be brought to the fore. It is from the persona of this emotion that we must lift the veil to encounter the raw instinct that demands attention. We know that we have come upon the correct interpretation when we feel a clearing of the mist, when we are no longer haunted by a feeling separating us from our beloved instinct that needs expression, understanding and care.

❖ Chapter Five

Ego, Instinct, Self and the Dream

It has become apparent to me that a most significant dream usually emerges during the third trimester of pregnancy. This dream is inevitably the one that holds the core of the remaining fears and ambivalences.

A secure environment has already been prepared through dealing with the myths, drawing the pictures, discussing your ambivalences. Now you are safely able to attend to your remaining psychological preparation for an easy birthing. In Leclaire method, a special session is scheduled, and the mother and the therapist extensively go through all the mother's associations to each word, name, phrase, color, each nuance within the dream. An interpretation of the dream is then made and discussed. This takes approximately three to six hours and may be done in three two-hour sessions.

The woman usually feels very relieved, very excited, and very free. Any depression that might be creeping up on her is usually worked through at this time. It has been my observation that the woman then has an entirely different pattern of dreaming, i.e., her dreams become exciting and anticipatory in preparation for the coming event. However, sometimes this third trimester dream is truly just the rim of the tip of the iceberg, and further problems and fears present themselves. The mother is usually very eager and willing to work this through, and greatly looks forward to her analytic dream work sessions. The unconscious is very caring. It seems as though the mind, body and spirit are striving for pre-birthing alignment. It's as though the unconscious is cooperating with the forty-week time frame. Rather than complicating the pregnancy by acknowledging the information erupting from the unconscious, this, I feel, is another preparatory stage of labour. It is the preparation and care given during this stage that allows for the gracious and gentle opening of the cervix.

Just as the imminent birth of your baby affords you a new hope, and a reconnection to the life force, so the dream process reconnects you to your own inner life force. It becomes a very exciting task to work with the dream process during pregnancy. Every fiber of your being desires to be conscious for the birthing. The manifest content of the dream, however, may engender the same ambivalence as the upcoming birth.

The easiest way to attend to the law of our nature and its reality is to follow the dream, the pathway to the unconscious, to our instincts. If we follow this direct path to our instinctual intelligence, we are safely assured of being guided toward attaining our full potential.

An instinct is an innate need in all of us. The instinct itself does not have a goal. The goal of the instinct must come from the rational/ intuitive process. That which makes an instinct advantageous to both the self and society is the connection to the creative energy, the acknowledgement of the instinctual soul. The improper expression of an instinct is the underlying cause of our psychic pain and much of our physical pain.

The unconscious embodies the true self, whereas the ego is the socialized self. Through the dream process we are able to reconcile the socialized self to the instinctual self. It is in the reconciliation of our culture to our instincts that we become unique. Rather than becoming our "self," many of us instead search for a culture that suits our ego .

When we allow the ego to impose itself upon us, we live in the shadow of our own truth. The only way to attain a higher development is to allow the ego and the unconscious to meet head on and to work out a new plan. The ego being an introjection from a parent, an authority figure, or our society in general is then projected. There is no healthy ego, only the acceptance or rejection of it. It is the reconciled self that is healthy. We need to accept certain parts of our ego and disregard that which is undesirable, that which is incongruent with our instincts. Now we can re-sculpt the ego and make its shape our own. When we have reconstituted our ego with our self, we are reconciled and no longer need to manifest ourselves in the world. We are in complete accord. We are manifest.

Most societal problems occur when the ego interacts instead of the self. Through the dream we can see the blocks between the ego and the instinct. In the connection with the spiritual instinct, we can gain an understanding and bring about a compatibility of all three. It is only then that the reconciled self can emerge unviolated. Our instincts make themselves known through our emotions and through pictorial images in our dreams and visualizations.

In the dream state we see the raw archetype (picture of our instincts). In a state of meditation or hypnosis we see the archetype softened by the soul.

In an awakened state we see the cultural archetype, which is usually not in accord with the instinctual archetype. The instinctual archetype cannot be named, because the very nature of the word used at once imposes a cultured archetype upon it. Since none of us can describe our own instinctual archetype without culturally impinging upon it, we therefore cannot articulate the pure archetype. We can only extrapolate its essence through our whittling away to the barest fragment our own individual cultures. We then arrive at an emotional knowing, an intuition of soul.

Thus, when we don't reconcile the ego, the instinct and the soul, we may pass on this unresolved experience genetically to our offspring. Perhaps three generations later we may have a cultural archetype emerging from what seems like nowhere. However, there isn't anything that evolves from nowhere, as there isn't a nowhere. This emerging archetype, however, doesn't seem to fit into what we know of that person. It is the instinct now tainted by an ancestor's unresolved ego/instinct/soul. After X generations, if there is not a reconciliation, perhaps this tainted instinct now becomes a part of the genetic code, now becomes manifest in the soul and the body.

A most difficult problem arises when one has a bleeding of the unresolved ancestral self into the present generational instinct. If the instinct is not pure, how can the self be?

If we define the soul as that which makes a thing what it is; and if the soul is the essence of being human, then the soul always remains all-knowing of itself. The answer, then, is that when one has a bleeding of the ancestral ego, one must much more strongly connect to the truth that lies in the so-called DNA of the soul. Through this deep connection to the soul/spirit, we shall once again be able to be in touch with our human instincts. It is from this place that we can again begin the process of emerging from our beings as ourself. The answer, then, seems not to rest in bigger and better and more and more action, but in less and less movement and more and more quietude. The grand mechanisms thrusting themselves upon our lives and our birthing are merely a greater masking of the bleeding into the nuclei.

It is important, then, that we pay homage to our dreams, to the rational/intuitive consciousness of our self rather than the automatic conscious behavior of our ego and the imposing patriarchal ego.

An instinct without being graced by the spirit is merely an impulse. When filtered through the spirit, it becomes an idea, which is perhaps why the Greeks defined idea as an image dropped on our heads by the Olympian gods.

The greater the intensity of the emotion, the less the resolve between the ego introjects and the instinct's impulse. The ego can observe, but has no true awareness of the observation. The ego, being an introject, is the most unconscious part of our being; the awareness comes through the mediation of the spirit.

When the conscious and unconscious mind are not in opposition to each other, the longitudinal and circular muscles of the uterus will not be in opposition, either. When a woman faces her shadow through her dreams, she can then experience the fullness of the light of her life and her child's life. Then she can live, not in her shadow, her mother's shadow, or her child's shadow; then she can live and birth with a tremendous sense of freedom and joy and light; then her uterus will work for itself, not against itself. Then all the fear of childbirth, and nurturing, and living, and playing, and loving are free to be expressed through words, through tears, through the gamut of emotions. After the emotions are addressed, an integration of the ego into the self becomes possible. Now we can forego the opposition of the ego to the self, of the uterus to itself.

The uterus can now work together with the easy and consistent opening of the cervix and the relaxation of the circular muscles to prepare for the parting of the vaginal curtains, thus making way for the wondrous debut of a new and beautiful individual. It is during pregnancy that you can make great strides in your own individuation as well as in recognizing and accepting your upcoming role as the facilitator of your child's individuation.

The free flow of your instinctual psyche through physiological relaxation of your body, and the spiritual and psychological relaxation of the unconscious allows for one of the greatest experiences of love and joy and freedom. The more readily the neck of the unconscious can be drawn back, can be retracted to allow for the presentation of the dream, to allow for the birthing of the unconscious material, the more readily the cervix can remain uninhibited in its dilation. To put it simply: A resistance to the presenting dream from the unconscious to the conscious becomes physically manifested during labor by a resistant cervix. Thus, there is tension at all points. Now painless natural functions turn into an extremely painful, unnatural and, in fact, abnormal function.

The awakening of the unconscious that invariably occurs in the third trimester of pregnancy calls forth a primitive defense reaction. Unless this defense system is addressed, aided and assisted through an analysis of the dream material, it is recorded as anxiety, fear, and pain by the laboring woman. In consideration of this, prevention is essential. A good example of this is Christina's dream work.

Assignment

1. Make a decision, if you will, to remain open and curious to your dream.

2. Purchase a special notebook for the recording of your dreams.

3. Decide when you would like to begin to remember your dreams.

4. On the date you have decided upon, have your notebook and pen or pencil next to your bed.

5. Follow the steps outlined in this chapter for remembering your dreams.

Remember: Bringing your feelings and your attitudes into conscious awareness cannot hurt you, but remaining in denial and fear can. Good Luck! Gently pat yourself on your back for being willing to take a risk.

❖ Chapter Six

Pain and the Psycho-Neuro-Hormonal Connection

It has been my observation that a woman, having worked through many of her fears and anxieties in analysis, often has a recurrence of these feelings during pregnancy.

The unconscious of most women seems very willing to emerge and to be integrated into the self at this time. During pregnancy a woman's emotions are rather surface and labile. As irrational as they may seem, oftentimes there is a logic to emotions which can lead us down a primrose path right into the window of the unconscious. Both emotions and our unconscious have a life of their own. It is important to rein them into focus.

It is at this time that a woman has an opportunity to make great strides in analysis or therapy, for she now approaches her own mother instinct, or lack of it. She may also be aware of her own inner child emerging almost as a sibling in rivalry with the child in utero. The pregnant mother needs as much nurturing now as her baby will when he/she arrives. She now begins to realize that she is at risk of having her partner transfer his libido upon another. She risks his anima being connected to his new daughter, or she risks her animus being connected to her new son.

During the first trimester of pregnancy, the mother regresses in many ways to a somewhat infantile state. You may find that you require more sleep than usual, just as your newborn will. You may become irritated by loud sounds, and certain smells and tastes will become offensive. The newborn infant is also profoundly touched by the slightest sensory input.

Psychoanalytic theory states that the mother's regression permits a fusion between the baby and the mother. During the last trimester of pregnancy, it is very advantageous for the mother to begin to let go of her fusion fantasies, and just allow for the acknowledgment that she has bonded with a very special person inside of her. However, this person is not a part of her. This baby is a separate individual who has both bonding needs and individuation needs that must be recognized and addressed. If you, as the mother, realize that you are the parent of the baby whom you are birthing, rather than thinking this child is a part of you, it is not so difficult to let go. The cord is cut, fusion with the placenta is cut, the fusion with the mother is severed, only to be replaced by a bonding (which is why it is so important for the baby to be placed in the mother's arms immediately and to remain there until after the arrival of the placenta and the cutting of the cord.)

It is early in the second trimester that the pregnant mother begins to redefine many of her relationships. Her own mother now becomes the approving or disapproving grandmother-to-be.

She is often once again the center of her mother's attention. The real apple of her mother's eye, however, is the gift they both await. If her mother is unavailable, the pregnant mother often feels the pain of her own unresolved dependency needs.

It is via the pattern of emotions that all the mother's conflicts emerge. These feelings must be acknowledged and explored in an open, nonthreatening, nurturing environment. Traditionally, the role of the obstetrician (the one who stands in front of) has been to deal with the technical, mechanical aspects of pregnancy rather than the psychological aspects. Through dream analysis and hypnosis sessions, the mother has a safe container in which to express that which threatens her.

It is as though the pregnant mother is having an emotional seizure and needs to be confined and guided through the work. For if her conflicts, fears and anger remain unconscious, they may be manifested through incomplete contractions, poor positioning of the baby for birthing, or in a variety of other complications.

It is during pregnancy that the father begins to experience his fears and anxieties. He begins to realize that all of man's creations are mere technological prestidigitations, and that a woman's creation is a profound miracle. Thus he begins to realize his own limitations. He is, for the most part, in my experience, less able to articulate these conflicts, these confinements. Perhaps to do so would make his boundaries seem all too real. Every human needs a certain amount of denial, and this we must respect.

Through the classes in the Leclaire method, the father has a safe forum in which to express and discuss his feelings if he so chooses. He now has a vehicle whereby he can grow and can expand his limitations. As the support person, it is he who guides the mother in the hypnotic trance. It is he who nurtures her throughout all the steps of labour. He learns how to care for himself, how to reinforce his own energy so that he can care for his partner and can help her to stay focused and relaxed.

He connects with the mother instinct in himself, thus rendering himself whole. It is when we connect with both our right and left brain that it becomes irrelevant what kind of genitalia we have, even in the throes of the manifestation of the greatest difference between man and woman. In fact, it is at this time more than at any other that man and woman can become as one, both working together as parents for the common goal of celebrating in a calm and joyous, nurturing way, the birth of their child.

It is at this time that the father can become the positive guiding voice. Through hypnotic suggestion, the mother lets go of her left brain critical activity. Here the father picks it up, making the judgment as to when it is necessary to deepen the hypnosis.

Now the father also connects to his own intuitive thought, seeing when his partner needs to be touched, needs to be encouraged, needs to be calmed, or needs to be reassured and complimented.

Through the process learned in the classes, the mother is able to come to terms with her baby's being a separate individual, an independent personality. Both mother and father learn that their child is dependent upon them for care, acceptance and acknowledgment of his or her need for independence. When the mother truly realizes this separateness, she is able to birth the baby with less discomfort and more freedom and celebration. When she realizes that she is not losing a part of herself, but rather that she is giving birth to an individual, she becomes less frightened and more accepting of the process, thus allowing herself the pleasure of an easy labour and birthing.

From the beginning, we must each follow our own path. It would stand to reason that if the mother were encouraged to know her own path and then give herself permission to follow it, she would allow her baby to do the same. The baby instinctively knows the correct and easiest path into his mother's arms. Perhaps it is the mother's ambivalence that alters that path. It is a time when the mother must be ego-less, must be aware of the child inside her belly, and must allow that child full rite of passage.

If the mother has not accepted her own self as an individual, how can she allow her unborn baby the courtesy of being his own person apart from her? If this baby is an extension of her own ego, her unfulfilled needs and desires, of the father's hope and dreams and the grandparents' fantasies, how can she birth without pain? The freer the woman is and the more courage she has demonstrated in getting to know herself, the more wonderful will be her pregnancy, labour and birthing. When pregnancy is enhanced by nurturing, and the problems that emerge are addressed in a direct and caring manner, and when the mother is given permission to understand and to continue with her work on her personal negative shadow, then the exhilaration of birth need not be diminished by unnecessary pain.

By recognizing the psycho-neuro-hormonal connection during pregnancy, as we have finally begun to do with premenstrual syndrome and postpartum depression, we can intervene early to prevent a crisis and to establish a healthy relationship to the emotional energy surrounding this blessed miracle.

Through the Leclaire method, both you and your partner can work together to clear your birth canal of all fear, and of all ambivalence, so that your baby can come through the curtain onto the vaginal stage with an easy rotation of his head.

What causes difficulties and complicated pregnancies? There is no definite answer. There are many different complications and thus many different causes applied to them. Some may come from an impaired belief system.

Exercise: Read the following:

Pain in childbirth is dependent upon:
1. Myths.
2. Incorporation of myths into one's own culture.
3. Acceptance of these myths with subsequent repression.
4. Adopting a belief system to one's own disadvantage.
5. Fear, anxiety, panic.
6. Nonbeneficial interpretation.

Comfort and Celebration of Life Force are dependent upon:
1. Myths.
2. Choosing of these positive myths that we want to incorporate into our culture.
3. Rejection of negative myths.
4. Analytic dream work.
5. Accepting the new and positive nature of our belief system.

Exercise:
A. At this point in time, on a scale of one to ten (ten being the most painful), how painful do you anticipate childbirth will be for you? 1 - 2 - 3 - 4 - 5 - 6 - 7 - 8 - 9 - 10 (circle one).
B. Is this an acceptable pain level for you? Yes - No
C. If your answer is no, look back over the five points of comfort and celebration of the life force and write out your beliefs around number one, and then write out the myths that would be more beneficial to your belief system and make a decision to do whatever it takes to alter your "myth" in order to bring you closer to your comfort zone.
D. Look at number four and do what it takes to remember and work on a dream in the next two to four weeks.
E. After you have completed steps A through D, take ten minutes to go off to your garden or to a gentle place in nature and address number five. You may do this by again writing out your desirable beliefs, this time in an affirmative form.

Example: I have accepted my ambivalence surrounding being a mother, and I have let go of my fear and judgment surrounding this ambivalence. It is normal to feel this way. The best that I can do is to become aware of my purpose in life, my need for support, play, and exercise, and to nurture myself in all these areas to the best of my ability. I have also opened myself to both physical and emotional help from wherever it flows. Taking care of myself to the best of my ability, I am now able to nurture my baby freely and willingly. I accept my own need for nurturance. I accept that I am a loving and fallible human being.

❖ Chapter Seven

Nutrition and Exercise

Another influence that you have over your physical well-being, and the well-being of your body and your baby, is through proper nutrition and through the avoidance of drugs (including alcohol and nicotine) by both you and your child's father. Through proper nutrition you can hinder disease and enhance health. There is an ongoing controversy surround supplementary vitamins and minerals. Many physicians and CNMs (Certified Nurse Midwives) feel that a well-balanced diet of natural foods provides the best balance of all the necessary nutrients, and that some vitamins and mineral supplements may even be harmful. Since there is such controversy over the use of supplements and the proper dosage, it certainly would not be harmful to discontinue all non-prescription drugs (including aspirin and nose drops) and vitamins two weeks prior to your attempt at conception. You can always resume a supplemental regime after checking with your obstetrician or nurse midwife.

To begin an exercise program of walking or swimming or yoga is also a good idea. It is important to maintain an exercise program during pregnancy, as research shows that regular exercisers usually have easier pregnancies and birthing than those who don't exercise. There is also a lower incidence of Caesarean births among women who exercise.

A regular exercise plan and a well-balanced natural food nutritional program, along with the rest of the Leclaire method, can prevent the mood swings of pregnancy, including post-partum depression.

During the first three months of pregnancy, you will find that you have many cravings, oftentimes for foods that are not very nutritious. I believe that nutrition in pregnancy deserves more than a chapter, therefore I highly recommend *Macrobiotic Pregnancy and the Care of the New Born* by Michio and Aveline Kushi. It is a comprehensive book that explains how to deal with all aspects of nutrition and cravings during pregnancy.

It is often very difficult to change our old behaviors. It is easier if we have a schedule and implement it one day at a time. If you are now exercising once a week — let's say you walk for ten minutes — and your belief is that you would benefit by walking twenty minutes, four days a week, then set a realistic goal week by week so you can build to your twenty-minute, five-day goal.

Example:

Week 1: I shall walk 20 minutes this week. Set day and time.

Week 2: I shall walk 20 minutes this week. Set day and time.

Week 3: I shall walk 20 minutes twice this week. Set time for second walk; do first walk at same time.

Week 4: I'll walk 20 minutes twice this week. Same time as last week.

Week 5: I'll continue to walk 20 minutes twice this week. Same time as last week.

Week 6: I'll walk 20 minutes three times this week. Schedule times and follow through.

Week 7: I'll continue 20 minutes, three times a week.

Week 8: I'll continue 20 minutes, three times a week.

Week 9: I'll continue 20 minutes, three times a week.

Week 10: I'll walk 20 minutes, four times this week.

Week 11: I'll continue 20 minutes four times this week.

Week 12: I'll continue 20 minutes four times this week.

Week 13: You have now reached your goal. It is now a habit, a part of your life. You may walk longer or more often, if you choose, but you can feel good about having met your goal if you continue at 20 minutes, four times a week. Congratulations!

YOUR EXERCISE GOAL

Set a realistic goal for yourself around exercise and use the blank graph which follows to schedule your progress. Be gentle with yourself. Never schedule more than five days. You may exercise six or seven days if you choose, but do not write down more than five. This allows room for an off day or weekend. It gives you the freedom not to be perfect, not to be too hard on yourself.

Week	Mon	Tues	Weds	Thurs	Fri	Sat	Sun
1							
2							
3							
4							
5							
6							
7							
8							
9							
10							
11							
12							
13							
14							
15							

Now let's look at nutrition in the same way. Let us assume that you are now eating three healthy meals per week out of a possible twenty-one. Your desired goal is to eat fifteen healthy meals per week. You're eating ten unhealthy snacks per week. Your goal is to eliminate all but two unhealthy snacks per week.

Week

1   Three healthy meals this week.

2   Three healthy meals this week, and I will browse in bookstore or library or health food store for books that I like on nutrition and pregnancy.

3   Four healthy meals this week, and I shall begin reading a book on nutrition and pregnancy.
4   Four healthy meals and continue to read book.
5   Four healthy meals. Finish book.
6   Four healthy meals. Go through cupboards and eliminate and toss unhealthy foods.
7   Five healthy meals. I'll begin to implement new ideas I've learned in the book.
8   Five healthy meals.
9   Five healthy meals. Eliminate one unhealthy snack and replace with healthy snack.
10   Six healthy meals this week.
11   Six healthy meals this week.
12   Six healthy meals this week.
13   Seven healthy meals this week. Eliminate two unhealthy snacks and replace with healthy snacks.
14   Seven healthy meals this week.
15   Seven healthy meals this week. Eliminate three unhealthy snacks; replace with healthy snack.

Continue at a reasonable pace until you are habitually eating fifteen healthy meals per week, and have eliminated all but two unhealthy snacks per week.

Again, choose a nutritional plan that makes sense to you, and then make a decision to follow your new beliefs. It is not always comfortable at first to change our habits, but the more we persist during the uncomfortable stage, the closer we are to reaching a new level of comfortableness in our desired healthy eating habits.

Make your goals easily attainable. Never set them too high. You do not want to fail. You want to succeed. Therefore, it is better to take your time, making sure that you are habitually at level one before you move on to the next level.

For example during the Lebanese Crisis in 1982, a midwest hamburger chain airlifted several thousand hamburgers for the American marines. It was really a publicity stunt, but it also symbolized a widespread recognition that adjusting to a new environment is difficult and that our desire for familiar foods persists when circumstances change.

The transition to a more natural diet and way of life should present no serious conflict. If we rush things and try to change overnight, we are bound to make mistakes, and within a short period we will resort to our former lifestyle. The desire for instant satisfaction is part of the modern consumer mentality. Give yourself permission to change slowly, gradually and consistently.

❖ Chapter Eight

What Hypnosis Is and Isn't

What is hypnosis?

Hypnosis is an altered state of consciousness. It is a normal state that occurs just as you are drifting into sleep. The brainwaves are said to be of an alpha wave deepening into a beta wave and can be differentiated by an electroencephalogram.

What does it feel like to be hypnotized?

Since hypnosis is a naturally occurring state that all people experience right before falling asleep, everyone can be hypnotized. However, not all people will allow themselves to be hypnotized, and many people are resistant to being hypnotized.

How can I overcome my resistance to hypnosis?

The first step is to understand why you are resistant. These resistances will usually be brought into consciousness through a dream. A thorough working of the dream between the mother and her analyst will aid in the awareness, understanding, acceptance, and letting go of the resistance. The second step is to practice, practice, practice.

What is the value of hypnosis during childbirth?

Through our program of rational/intuitive birthing with hypnosis, the brain is being taught to receive relearning stimuli. During the inhibitory phase you are pretty much unaware of what is going on around you. The awareness of a narrow range of stimuli is engaged by the hypnotist, who then calls to your attention specific ideas. The great benefit derived from using hypnosis during childbirth is that it enhances, and normalizes, the natural physiology of labour and birth by reducing tension. The hypnotic state helps to maintain and assure the flow of oxygen to the foetus. Hypnosis eliminates the anxiety which can cause diminished oxygen flow.

Why do you use music in the training classes?

It has been found that the slow movement (largo) of the baroque concertos has a rhythm of sixty beats per minute. This is like the beat of a slow and steady pulse. When this beat is played, your body relaxes and your mind becomes concentrated on the task at hand. This is just another tool that we use to facilitate relaxation and concentration.

Do we learn self-hypnosis in the classes?

All hypnosis is self-hypnosis. The hypnotist is really just a facilitator in the process in the same fashion as the midwife or doctor is the facilitator of the birth process. Neither the doctor nor the midwife delivers the baby. The baby is birthed by the mother. The hypnotic facilitator becomes better at helping the mother to induce hypnosis when she is in a trance or in a relaxed state herself. It is at this time that she is more in touch with her right brain, her intuitive knowledge. One is more apt to flow into an alpha state when the energy field of a person is in a relaxed alpha state, which is one of the reasons why the fathers are also trained in hypnosis techniques. If they are in alpha, they can more readily act as a conduit to hypnosis.

Can hypnosis be dangerous to the mother or to the foetus?

Quite the contrary. When a mother is stressed, adrenaline is released, thus allowing the catecholamines to cross the placental barrier, which, in turn, gives the baby a stress cue.

Conversely, when a mother uses hypnotic techniques and is able to drift into a pre-sleep state, she sends soothing messages across the placental barrier. By the sixth month, the cortex of the baby's brain is able to take in messages and to retain them. It is advantageous to the mother to be relaxed and to send soothing messages to the foetus.

How does hypnosis work?

Hypnosis works through suggestions. Our minds are constantly given suggestive stimuli, both from the external world and from our own internal world. These suggestions have created both good and bad habits. In hypnosis we attempt to replace the negative stimuli with positive stimuli. If we see the mind, the body, the spirit, and our emotions as a quartet, then we can perhaps see that the harmony of each is a necessary accompaniment to their unity. If the spirit is peaceful, we can then have beautiful mental visions of a joyous birth, thus allowing pleasurable emotions. These pleasurable emotions help to maintain the neuromuscular harmony of the body. If the muscles of the body are relaxed, we are more readily able to avail ourselves of positive and relaxed mental images, and in turn, the relaxed mental images permit the association of pleasurable sensations and emotions. All of this serenity on a physical plane allows us to get in touch with the endless peace within our spirit.

There seems to be a correlation between emotions and muscle tension. Since the goal of hypnosis in childbirth is to decrease (and when the mother and support person are willing, to eliminate) the discomforts of labor, our first task is to eliminate tension in all involved peripheral parts and to relax all the muscle groups.

When the body is relaxed, fear is an unwelcome visitor. Fear and relaxation are incongruent, thus the muscles of the uterus, used to expel the baby, are given little resistance from the relaxed body. So, whether we start with the body, the mind, the spirit, or the emotions, relaxed and pleasant actions and images influence the fulfillment of a relaxed and joyous birth.

When and how should I begin my hypnosis training?

It is advantageous to being the first hypnotic session early in pregnancy. This helps the mother to prevent morning sickness, and it helps her to remain in optimum health by beginning to address and to relieve her fear and stress. Although most women are very open to learning hypnosis/visualization techniques and are eager to receive the benefits, some are naturally more receptive than others. Thus, it is recommended that each mother is seen privately for at least one session prior to the group meeting. This session should be as early as possible and preferably no later than twenty weeks.

In this session we discuss your lifestyle, your feelings about pregnancy, childbirth and motherhood. We also discuss your relationship to your partner and/or your feelings about not having a partner. We also cover any particular fears, complications and individual needs. Then we proceed to the first hypnosis session.

What are the behavioral manifestations of hypnosis?

First there is a visible release of tension with slight involuntary movements of the extremities as they begin to relax. There is a deepening of the breath.

After the muscles release, the breathing becomes slower, more regular and shallow, the eyelids close, eye movements slacken, an occasional smile passes across the face, and tears can be released. You will feel an opening of your body and a relaxation of your jaw and your perineum. Anesthesia can be developed by suggestion, first in the hand and then in other parts of the body, if so desired. After sufficient practice, the hypnotic state can be maintained with eyes opened in a state of somnambulism, i.e., walking about and following suggestions without affecting the trance state. This is important during the early stage of labour, when it is often more comfortable to be up and around.

I hear a lot of talk about breathing during labour. How will hypnosis teach me how to breathe properly?

Hypnosis will keep you relaxed during labour. A relaxed body knows exactly how to breathe. A relaxed body always inhales and exhales properly, adapting totally to the situation at hand. Relaxing hypnotically helps you to stay in the moment, to stay with the self rather than engaging in the critical faculties of the ego. When you hear something funny, you spontaneously laugh, you don't ask yourself how to do it. Through mastery of the hypnotic techniques, your mouth will be relaxed and your breathing will be spontaneously perfect. You will automatically inhale through your nose, gently and deeply when necessary. You will feel as though you are exhaling through your vagina and/or your rectum.

I thought my uterus was supposed to contract during labour. If hypnosis relaxes my muscles and my uterus is a muscle, isn't that dangerous?

The uterus has three muscle layers. All of these muscles need to work in harmony to allow for an easy and relaxed birth. One layer shortens and tightens, thus pushing the baby downwards and out of the uterus. The second layer controls the blood supply, and the third and inner layer keeps the outlet opened. The relaxation of the mother facilitates all this happening. If there is no cooperation, then the third layer acts in opposition to the first, and the outlet closes, thus inhibiting the progress of the foetus through the birth canal. Now we have a problem. The muscles in opposition are experienced as tension. Fear causes more tension and thus more pain, resulting in further inhibition of progress.

It is within this cycle that maternal and foetal distress can occur. One of the main tasks of hypnosis is the prevention of the undesirable cycle; for it is here that the tension manifests itself as a resistance to the birth. Any resistance to the birth is manifested by more tension, further inhibition of labour and a "tight-lipped cervix." Hypnotic relaxation permits the free circulation of the blood through the middle layer of the muscles, which in turn allows the necessary oxygen to the working muscles, which helps to keep the baby in a non-stressed, relaxed state during his or her journey out of the birth canal.

When an hypnosis trained mother experiences uterine contractions, she can relax her cervix, thus preventing the need for stronger uterine contractions. When an hypnosis trained mother experiences deep pressure and stretching, she is able to relax into her pelvic floor, she is able to inhale through her nose or mouth and send the breath right through her cervix, out through her rectum or vagina in anticipation of the oncoming head.

Why is it important for the fathers to attend the hypnosis and childbirth classes?

Many fathers respond to the woman's increased intimacy needs (not to be confused with sexual needs, which are often decreased during pregnancy) as an unnecessary demand and drain on their time and energy. This reaction evokes feelings of abandonment, fear and helplessness in the mother, all of which are expressed to the foetus via the placental circulation.

By educating the fathers as to how they play an integral and important part in the birthing process, and by helping them to realize the importance of their participation, we establish a new expression of harmony toward the unborn child. Now the joy of pregnancy, labour and birthing can begin, for they are all working together as a team. The father will have connected to his positive mother instinct, nurturing himself and his wife in turn, and together they are nurturing their baby.

It is at this time that many childhood fears re-emerge. It is also at this time that the father's fear of his new role surfaces. Both the mother and the father learn that they are not alone in their anxieties. Hopefully, they have learned to trust the group and the leader, and are able to accept the support and understanding that is necessary to deal with these emotions. Through the father's connection to his own nurturing self, he gets to experience a new kind of inner strength. The stress of pregnancy, instead of being a burden to the father and a period of isolation and loneliness for the mother, is transferred into a shared growth experience through which they each can learn an inner sense of balance.

As part of the training, the fathers also become hypnotic subjects. Both the mothers and the fathers enjoy this relaxation and the time away from the stress of their usual roles. By being hypnotized, the fathers become better able to help the mothers into an hypnotic state. It gives the fathers a great sense of comfort to know that they can have such a profound and relaxing effect on their partner.

Often the fathers joke with each other, "I think I'll keep her in this state and have her wait on me, hand and foot." Everyone laughs, but this is truly an important connection for the man.

In some sense he is looking for reassurance that his partner will still be nurturing to him when the baby arrives. Many mothers say that under usual circumstances they would not feel comfortable abandoning themselves in this way to their partner. However, the pregnancy and imminent birth create a need in the woman to be taken care of, to be nurtured, to be intimate and to be relaxed and free from pain. The need in the father is to be needed, to be competent, and to be able to expand his limitations.

So the hypnosis classes relieve them both of their fear and tension surrounding childbirth. It allows the mother to enter into labour completely relaxed, calm and serene in her knowledge that her body knows exactly how to birth their baby with a minimum of discomfort. The mild hypnotic state is also an advantageous position for the father as support person. Through hypnosis, he is able to remain calm, competent and energized. Through the father's participation in the classes during pregnancy and through his support during labour and birthing, he is able to significantly contribute to the quality of his partner's pregnancy, labour, and birthing process.

❖ Chapter Nine

Hypnosis Techniques

Cover yourself with at least a light blanket, as it is not uncommon to feel chilly. You may have your support person read these instructions to you aloud, in a soft voice, and at a very, very slow pace.

1. The easiest way to relax a muscle is to first exaggerate its contraction. The easiest way to relax the diaphragm is to focus in exhaling. You begin the relaxation by first getting in any comfortable position.

2. The second step is to observe your breathing. Don't alter it in any way, just observe it. Now place one of your hands on your lower abdomen. Inhale through your nose. Try to blow your abdomen up like a balloon; fill it with air. Feel your hand rise. Now blow the breath out through your mouth with three slow blowing-type breaths, then relax your breathing and focus on it. Again, observe your breathing, but don't alter it in any way. (When we breathe normally, when awake, we don't usually have a great rise and fall of the abdomen; it is usually the chest and shoulders that rise.) This deep breathing is different from our usual inhalation. Inhale a second time through the nostrils, filling the abdomen with air, feeling the hand rise with the abdomen, again blowing the breath out through the mouth with three soft blowing breaths. Again, relax your breathing. Observe it, don't alter it in any way.
   Now take another deep breath, filling the abdomen with air, and blow it out through the mouth softly and slowly. This time, paying specific attention to your exhalation, breathe out completely, sending

the breath out through your rectum and/or your vagina. Repeat this inhalation one more time.

3. Turn your focus toward your feet and ankles. Gently contract your feet and ankles; now contract them a bit more and now relax them.

Contract your calves, shins and knees gently and then firmly, as tightly as you can, and now release them. Let go of all the tension in your lower legs.

Turn your focus toward your thighs, buttocks and genital area. Contract these areas gently, firmly, and now as tightly as you can. Relax your thighs, let go of all tension in your thighs, your buttocks, your genital area. Again, focus on your breathing; don't alter it in any way, only observe it.

Focus on your abdomen and all of its contents. Become aware specifically of your uterus and your baby. Take a large, slow, deep abdominal breath and exhale it to your belly, to your uterus, to your baby, out your rectum and/or your vagina. Let a deep sense of relaxation and peace float across your belly.

Now become aware of your spine. Begin to contract one vertebra at a time and let the tension spread out from your spine across your back and up your sides until your entire back is arched with tension.

Feel the force of gravity pulling the tension out of your back and into the ground. Let go of all the tension in your back and feel yourself sinking comfortably into the bed or chair.

Become aware now of your chest, your breasts, and contract them gently and relax them; contract them again gently, and then relax them again.

Now contract your neck, right and left, and front and back, and let go of the tension in your neck; let it relax.

Begin to contract your shoulders, your upper arms, elbows, lower arm, wrists, hands, fingers, and make fists with your hands. Now extend your arms and spread your fingers as wide apart as you can.

Relax your shoulders, arms and hands; take a deep breath and send the breath down your spine. Take another deep abdominal breath and send it down your arms. Feel yourself letting go of all tension in your body.

Now we come to the head and face, the most important relaxation. Many of us hold tension in our jaw. Clench your jaw for a moment and observe the tension beginning to return to the rest of your body. Now relax your jaw and let your mouth fall open. Turn your attention toward your scalp, your hair follicles, your forehead, your eyebrows, your eyelids, the area around your eyes, your temples, your cheekbones, your jaw, your chin, your ears, your nose, your nostrils, your lips, your tongue, your gums and teeth, the mucous membrane lining of your mouth, your throat. Now swallow, and scrinch your entire face up like a prune; harder now, tighter, clench your jaw. Now let it all go. Relax your face, feel the weight and the heaviness in your eyelids. Let them remain comfortably closed.

Now, with your mouth slightly open, begin to scan your body with your mind's eye to locate any areas of your body that are still tense. Now contract those areas of your body that are still tense and slowly relax them. Take a deep abdominal breath and send the breath to those areas and then out through your rectum and/or your vagina.

4. Once again, just focus on your breathing, not altering it, just observing it. Now begin to visualize a staircase of ten steps. You may design them any way you want, you may place them anywhere you want. Some woman like to climb down into a comfortably safe and shallow pool of water where they can float, a place where, if possible, it might be comfortable to birth your baby.

Now begin to climb the staircase, counting to yourself and having your support person count you down.

10   down
9   and deeper, deeper and down
8   deeper, now, down deeper
7   your arms and legs feel totally relaxed
6   deeper and deeper and down, all sounds other than your support person's voice are out of your awareness. If any other sounds enter into your consciousness, they will only serve to deepen your state of relaxation, peace and serenity.

5   deeper now, down deeper
4   your face and jaw are totally relaxed
3   deeper and deeper and down
2   your eyelids are very, very heavy; you could open them if you wanted to, but you don't really want to open them.
1   feeling totally comfortable and centered, better than you have felt in a long, long time.

5. Now turn your attention to the area between your two eyebrows and, with your eyes closed, look into this area, also known as your third eye.

[The support person can now be quiet for a minute while the mother begins to center herself and relax herself even more deeply through her focusing into the third eye.]

Now the support person may continue to read:

The work and practice of looking into the third eye is most important, as it is the place of deepest relaxation. It is within this point that you are to focus while you are pushing. If you can relax during the contractions of the first stage of labour, and if you can relax in between the contractions during the second stage, and if you can look deeply into your third eye, relaxing your jaw, keeping your eyes closed and pushing from deep within your third eye, your circular muscles will be loose and relaxed and childbirth will progress normally and naturally.

You will have a great sense of your labour paying off, you will have a great sense of accomplishment. Through your third eye, you get in touch with your body's perfect knowledge of how to birth your baby. Your body knows exactly what to do, how to push, when to push, how to breathe, when to inhale, when to exhale. All you have to do is to practice, practice, practice, and to trust your body's intuition and stay relaxed. Once you have engaged the critical faculties of your mind, you are no longer experiencing the moment, you are no longer trusting your body's perfect knowledge. All you have to do is tell yourself, "I want to relax, I don't want to think, I want to focus on my third eye. It is beneficial for me to believe, to know that I can birth my baby in a comfortable and relaxed manner. I am willing to work hard to push when I need to do so; I will lose myself in my work. I am relaxed now, I am more deeply relaxed than I've been in a long, long time."

Now begin to project way out into the universe a big ball of crimson red light. As you look at the light, it comes closer and closer and closer until it fades away, leaving you looking once again into your third eye.

Now project way out into the universe a big ball of violet light. It, too, begins to come closer and closer and closer until it fades away; again you are looking into your third eye, this time more deeply than before.

Now project way out into the universe a big ball of emerald green light, and as it gently bounces toward you, it fades away. This time you are looking more deeply, more peacefully into your third eye.

Deeper and deeper into your third eye, you relax deeply into it. Now project way out into the universe a big ball of orange light. Closer and closer it comes to you until it fades, and now you are peacefully, blissfully back into the serenity of your third eye. You are becoming more and more familiar with the omniscience within you.

You enjoy the depth and the peace. Now you project way out into the universe a big ball of yellow light. It is splendid out there. It comes in closer and closer, and gently fades away. You are deeply centered and you look into your third eye. A great sense of peace and comfort and courage fill your being.

Now you project way out into the universe a big ball of blue light. This ball of light is different from the others. As it comes close to you, it bursts into a magnificent, warm, healing white light, much like the healing, soothing rays of the sun. The white light begins to surround you, envelop you and soothe you even more. You feel caressed by it. It begins to flow down through the top of your skull, down through the medulla oblongata, down your spine to the base of your spine, and when it reaches the base of your spine, the healing white light begins to radiate throughout all of your extremities. It flows down through your right hip, and leg, and foot, and toes, and through your left hip, leg, foot and toes. It flows down through your shoulders, into your arms, through your wrists, and into your hands and fingertips. The white healing light now begins to fill your chest cavity, and fill your heart with a warmth and a love and an acceptance of yourself that you haven't felt in a long time.

The healing white light flows out of your heart into your abdomen. It surrounds your uterus, and penetrates your uterus and lines the walls of your uterus with a healing white light. The light surrounds your baby and places your baby in the proper birthing position. It helps your baby to grow normally, naturally, comfortably and healthily. It relaxes the baby and tells the baby that you are a calm, loving, and nurturing mother. You will be able to use the white light as an ally during pregnancy, labour, birthing, and postpartum.

In this state of deep relaxation, make a circle on your chest with the middle finger of your left hand. This is called an anchor. Whenever your use this anchor during labour, you will immediately become deeply relaxed.

If you begin to have an anxiety attack, or begin to feel pain during labour, all you need to do it use your anchor. Make a circle on your chest with the middle finger of your left hand and say:
I am beginning to feel pain, and I don't want to feel any pain. I am going to make a circle on my chest five times and focus on my third eye, and I will again be pain-free and in an alpha state. I will feel no discomfort and no anxiety. I will visualize the white light present within. It is my ally. I am filled with peace, hope and comfort. I am again relaxed and able to go with the flow of my body. I am again able to celebrate the birthing of my baby.

You may repeat this technique any time you or your support person feel that you are no longer in an alpha state. Always remember to allow your exhalations to be complete, breathing through the contractions and out through your rectum and/or your vagina.

❖ Chapter Ten

Techniques to Deepen Hypnotic State

1. Make a circle on your chest, and continue to make it until your arm falls loosely to your side. You are then very relaxed.

2. To deepen your relaxation even more: begin to examine the fingers of your left hand. First the thumb -- note the detail of your skin, the joints, the nail. Move on to the index finger, the middle finger, the ring finger, and the pinky. Now slowly open and close your fingers, then take your entire hand and slowly, very, very slowly. move it toward your third eye. When you touch your third eye with a fingertip of your left hand, you will be in a very, very deep state of relaxation.

If you like to continue working with the left hand, you may go on to the glove anesthesia technique.

3. Now visualize your putting your left hand into a bucket of ice cold water. You begin to experience tingling and numbness, and then your hand becomes heavy and without any feeling at all. You have absolutely no sensation in your left hand. Now strike your left hand with the middle finger of your right hand. Your left hand feels totally limp and relaxed and without sensation. You cannot feel the middle finger of your right hand touching your left hand.

Now you can practice transferring this glove of anesthesia to your abdomen and perineum, so that you will have one more tool in case you begin to think about fear and pain. In case you become anxious or experience some discomfort in your abdomen or perineum, you can now place this gloved hand there, and provide yourself with another comfort tool, another relaxation tool for remaining centered and in touch with the miraculous knowledge within your body. Now you may focus even more deeply into your third eye.

4. Here is another technique that seems to be the particular favorite of women. When the contractions are the most intense, the support person puts his/her hand very firmly around your left ankle and squeezes. Rather than focusing on your contractions, you now focus on your third eye and send the white light to your ankle. It is very difficult to feel more than one pressure at the time; thus, if you focus on your third eye and send an intensity of white light to your ankle, you will not be aware of your contractions; rather, you will be aware of an intensity of white light where the pressure occurs about your ankle.

Practice this now. It is a good idea to practice this entire procedure with your support person once a week. It is a good idea for you to play your hypnosis and childbirth tape four times a week, starting as early in pregnancy as possible.

I also recommend your becoming familiar with the music that you might choose to play during your labour and birthing. Some women prefer silence. However, since I use music in our training sessions (after the induction takes place), many of the mothers and their support persons have paired this music with deep relaxation and a feeling of confidence and safety. The music is very specific and has been chosen because it slows body rhythms to more efficient levels.

It's a good idea to begin hypnosis as soon as the contractions begin. This helps to keep things relaxed from the beginning. This also helps the support person to realize his/her role from the onset.

If you are not having your baby at home, on the way to the hospital you may play your hypnosis tape. Be certain to use earphones as you do not want your driver to hear the hypnotic suggestions and fall asleep at the wheel. Under hypnosis, you may tell yourself, or your support person may tell you, that you may open your eyes and walk about and be aware of that which you need to be aware of for safety and navigation. Any time you want to go back into a deeper state, you may use your anchor, the circle on your chest. Any time you want to focus or want to be more alert, yet very concentrated on the task at hand, you may play your music tape very softly in the background.

❖ Chapter Eleven

Music and Healing

"I despise a world which does not intuitively feel that music is a higher revelation than all wisdom and philosophy."

Ludwig Von Beethoven

The Egyptians felt that music affected humans both by creating a physical sensation and by arousing a mental state somewhat similar to enchantment. The Chinese felt that music had a magical influence and was able to sustain Universal Harmony. They also felt, however, that if used improperly it could influence so greatly that it could destroy the harmony. To create harmony of mind, body and spirit, the ancients used music. Many cultures used music for healing, and the ancient Greeks honored Apollo as both the god of healing and of music. In the Old Testament we learn that it is the playing of musical instruments that heals King Saul's psychotic depression.

Just as pain requires awareness and attention, so does sound. When we hear a sound, it also has a memory component to it. In the background I now hear chirping birds, a flute and guitar sonata on my stereo, some vague carpentry sounds, and my dog licking herself constantly. Each of these sounds affects me physically, emotionally and spiritually. The birds make me clear-headed and relaxed; the music uplifts me and fulfills some of my spiritual needs; the carpentry, as it is in the distance, arouses a very pleasant and soothing memory of a childhood summer long gone. Molly, the dog, constantly licking herself, is, fortunately, mostly in the background. When I attend to it and it becomes foreground, I become irritated, my breathing becomes more rapid, and I am unable to concentrate.

The purpose of using music during pregnancy and in preparation for labour and birthing are: certain kinds of music relax us physiologically and help us to focus on the present in a positive way. It is this music that we use during pregnancy — the long, slow movements of the baroque concertos. When played in conjunction with deep relaxation, the largo movements create a memory pathway that we now automatically associate with physiological relaxation and positive emotional feelings. This music is aesthetically very pleasing, and it is also spiritually fulfilling. Thus, it enhances the alignment process of mind, body, and spirit, which is essential for a joyous and pain-free birth.

While the body is in a deep state of relaxation, the music enables the mind to concentrate on the task at hand. The mind/body is thus able to function at maximum efficiency, with the brain waves being maintained between 7 and 13 C.P.S. (cycles per second) (alpha wave).

The combination of this state and the music can facilitate the flow of energy throughout the body, thus eliminating the emotional stress and fear that can cause pain.

Aristotle wrote:
...emotions of any kind are produced by melody and rhythm; therefore by music a man becomes accustomed to feeling the right emotions; music has thus power to form character, and the various kinds of music based on the various modes may be distinguished by their effects on character — one, for example, working in the direction of melancholy, another of effeminacy; one encouraging abandonment; another self control; another enthusiasm, and so on through the series.

If the air vibrations of sound are capable of shattering glass and causing nausea and headache, it can perhaps also "soothe the savage..." of the unconscious and allow for a more relaxed and peaceful state of being, or as the Chinese stated, music can balance the vital energies. Music is the midwife between the physical body and the spiritual self. Therefore, it is advantageous to listen to music that elevates us to a state in which we want to be. Since childbirth is miraculous and should be joyous, certainly we would not like to be influenced by the music of a mechanistic composer. Rather, it would be beneficial to listen to music throughout pregnancy that is uplifting and reaching toward the sublime.

Much of the music of the twentieth century is mechanistic and materialistic. Pregnancy and birthing have been handled in just such a manner. Perhaps by moving toward sounds that are spiritual, we can reconnect to that aspect of the self. We must place our own value on our experiences in life and not be manipulated by the mechanistic culture in which we live, just because it is expedient for the technicians who attend to us. Perhaps to arrive at a resolution within our own self we should use all the tools that we can. As our dreams tell us of our self, our center, our soul, so the music that we play can facilitate that journey.

Beethoven's Fifth Symphony raises the question of worldliness and resolves it into the selection of that which is spiritual. During the final trimester, why not fill the air with the five final string quartets of Beethoven? Certainly these quartets can lead us to the joy and serenity and alignment of mind, body and spirit that is so imperative for an easy and joyous birthing.

The study of plant growth under certain kinds of music seems to reconcile the belief that music is objectively good for us or bad for us; that is, if we believe that the growth and proliferation of plants under the influence of Bach, and the withering and ultimate death of plants subjected to rock music, are inherently good and bad effects of music. A similar study was done with rats that were placed in identical mazes with a connecting bridge to each. When Bach was piped into the right maze and rock music into the left, all the rats hovered in the Bach box. The music now reversed, and the rats scurried from the right rock box over to the new Bach box. No one knows exactly what the rats felt, but it seems that they experienced some kind of pain when they heard rock, and an absence of pain or perhaps pleasure or comfort when they heard and felt Bach. It appears, then, that certain tunes are life enhancing, while certain other tonal combinations are detrimental to the life force.

A preliminary study has been executed with bacteria, finding that they die under some musical conditions and multiply under others.

If the joy of life comes with the alignment of mind, body and spirit, certainly music is the perfect vehicle for arriving at this joy.

Through the recommended music, your mind is engaged, thus concentration becomes automatic; the heart rate, regulated by the rhythm, reaches its natural state, and the sweetness of the music fills the heart with the tenderness appropriate for the miracle of birth. The composition of the music also calls forth the spirit, thus bringing into play all of the aspects necessary to connect to the joy of life. As Solomon said, there is nothing new under the sun. In each age we rediscover the same truths in a way in which they will be able to accommodate themselves into our society and our belief systems. The ancient cultures felt that all disease was an imbalance and that music, in proper tonal combinations, was capable of healing all ills. Through music one's entire being can be exalted, and therein lies the fulfillment of life.

When a society lives in a certain condition for a long length of time, that condition becomes an unconscious way of life. Pain and childbirth and anguish in it have been imposed upon women of our Western culture for a long, long time. For many women, to have a pain-free childbirth is a dream, a complete unreality. Many women want to get out of that belief system, but are holding on to it in some part of their unconscious.

I am working with a young woman in her 30's who had cancer and was having terrible side effects from her chemotherapy, one being an inordinate amount of pain caused by the shots she was receiving. Thus, the pain was caused by the body, but was being held by the mind. Usually the pain of childbirth is caused by the mind and is held by the body. Since Candace's mind was unwilling to receive the bodily pain, she was able to act in such a way that she would be able to eliminate the pain. She felt she needed a mild tranquilizer, as the pathway had already been established. "As soon as I awaken on the day I am to receive these injections, I am anxious, fearful, tearful and angry." Candace was able to use hypnosis to alter these pathways; however, upon arriving at the hospital, she met with two of her fellow patients who had just received the shots, and they began to say that they were worse each week. Not wanting to risk being in pain, Candace asked appropriately for outside assistance, a good step toward her getting well process.

Upon exploration, we arrived at the realization that she felt that some of the side effects, the high fever and chills, were important to her belief system of getting well, of having the chemotherapy work in a beneficial way. They are symptoms she wants to keep. However, she felt that the pain was unwarranted and had no correlation to the efficacy of her treatment. Therefore, she was able to take care of herself and vehemently request a mild sedative when the set of painful injections were given to her. After taking care of herself in this positive and assertive way, she began to be open to eliminating pain from the other areas of her life.

Disharmony can cause illness and pain, thus it is harmony that provides the cure. Perhaps the saying, "as in music, so in life," can come to pass. It may be difficult to change our belief systems overnight, but the peace, serenity, and harmony provided by "good" music is automatic.

Exercise:

Play your baroque music tape at least once a week during pregnancy, throughout labor, and while nursing your baby.

◆ Chapter Twelve

Recent Herstory

Margaret Ann

I chose the Leclaire method for the birth of my second child because I wanted to have more control of my birth experience. The first time had been wonderful, but very overwhelming. I had pre-term labour with my first pregnancy and had spent the last three months in bed, taking terbutaline every two hours. I was told by my doctors that I had a fifty percent chance of having the same thing happen with my second pregnancy. So we decided to try Leclaire to deal with the pre-term labour aspects before preparing for the birth.

I started using hypnosis in my fourth month. After the amniocentesis, mild contractions had started. I felt the baby was already too low, and while the contractions had not yet changed my cervix — I was being monitored very closely by my doctors — the symptoms were all depressingly similar to the first pregnancy.

We started with what became a familiar routine. I would lie down and relax my body by tightening and releasing it, starting with my feet. Next would come an image of a descending staircase (a part of the Leclaire method) — mine was grass-covered railroad ties in the side of a hill. Then came a walk up the mountain and into the garden. I kept debating whether to put a bench in my garden. Sometimes I had one, but it was never right. I finally ended up lying on the grass.

Then came the suggestions. "I have no need of any unnecessary contractions. Anne Marie is fine." We knew the baby was a girl and had already named her. "Anne Marie will go to term."

The week after the first session, my depression lifted. I felt positive for the first time about this pregnancy. Anne Marie seemed to be up higher, and I felt no more low pressure. And no contractions at all for five days.

For several months, the contractions remained normal. That is to say, the contractions I had did not affect my cervix. My doctors were pleased, but skeptical, when I told them I was doing hypnosis.

In my eighth month everything was put to the test. I experienced bleeding and ended up in the hospital. A small part of the placenta had come away from the wall of my uterus, but the bleeding stopped within twenty-four hours. However, it brought on many contractions, and my doctors did not want me to leave unless the contractions were under control. The same medication, terbutaline, was suggested.

I wanted none of it. I lay there listening to the monitor click off contractions every five minutes, and tried to gain some control. The nurse came in with the first dose, and I told her I was using hypnosis and that I thought I could stop the contractions — just give me half an hour. She allowed me fifteen minutes.

I tried to give myself the Leclaire method suggestions, to walk down the stairs, to go up the mountain and into the garden, to visualize white light surrounding the baby. It didn't work. Every time I felt myself relaxing, a wave of anxiety would crash over me and I was back to where I started, the monitor clicking away.

I called my husband, Pete, at home and asked him to come help me. As soon as he started talking to me, I relaxed. And the needle on the monitor dropped to a lower level on the tape. Pete talked me through all the suggestions, and I didn't have another contraction for forty minutes. A half an hour went by before the next one. The nurse took the tape away to show the doctor, and I was sent home without drugs. I could control the contractions.

Then, at the end of my pregnancy, we finally got around to using the hypnosis to prepare for the actual labour and delivery. Now the suggestions focused on my body changing for the birth. I visualized the white light as warm and soothing. I saw myself opening up, riding the crest of each contraction.

The only image that didn't work for me was to imagine a woman giving birth in the garden place that I went to after descending the stairs. I put her in there, and then found her intrusive. I needed to imagine my birth experience from the inside out, and I couldn't seem to use this image. But once she was in the garden, I couldn't get her out. She may be there still, quietly giving birth among the ferns under the birch trees by the stream.

I practiced every day with a Leclaire tape with new suggestions. "My birth is going to go exactly as it should. With every contraction I am opening up. Anne Marie is fine." Sometimes Pete made the suggestions. Ever since the experience in the hospital, I had come to rely on his voice helping me to relax, helping me to concentrate.

Some days I didn't feel really focused. Some days near the end, I didn't do the exercises at all. I was tired of being pregnant, tired of the whole experience.

But I went to term. For someone who has experienced the anxiety of pre-term labour, it is a triumph. The night before my due date, I started labour around four in the morning. The first contraction woke me up. It was strong and it hurt. I suddenly doubted my ability to use this hypnosis stuff. But I got out the tape recorder and put the headphones on while Pete lay beside me in the dark. Around five, we got up. The contractions were very strong, every five to ten minutes. I walked around, calm and pleased to finally be at this point. I hung on Pete's neck for each one, allowing my body to relax, picturing myself opening up like a rose, seeing the white light surrounding the baby.

At six o'clock it became apparent that soon we would need to go to the hospital. The contractions were regular and very strong, every five minutes. I felt in control. It wasn't that each one didn't hurt, but I was not overwhelmed by them. I felt I was working actively to get Anne Marie out.

At the hospital I refused the wheelchair and walked to the elevator, stopping to hold the railings and breathe and visualize. I did not want to get into bed and be monitored. As long as I was on my feet I was helping in an active way. But I did want to find out how dilated I was. I was five centimeters. That felt great. Half my labour was over in two hours.

At seven the doctor came and abruptly broke my water. I went from five to ten centimeters in five contractions. The jump in intensity was too much. I abandoned the effort to keep the white light visualized and just held onto the top of the bed. But that was transition, and it was very brief. In a few minutes I was pushing my daughter out. I started and stopped pushing when the doctor told me to — it just felt like another hypnotic suggestion — and we eased her head out without my having an episiotomy. Anne Marie was born at 7:10 a.m. She was nine pounds, nine ounces, and very healthy. I was in the hospital less than an hour, and my whole labour, from start to finish, was a little over three hours.

The decision to use the Leclaire Method was a good one for us. I believe that it kept me from having pre-term labour, and it kept me off the terbutaline. It brought my husband and myself closer together. And although I didn't use it in transition, I believe it was the reason my labour progressed so rapidly. If nothing else, using hypnosis gave me a strong sense of well-being during my pregnancy and my delivery.

And the funny thing is that I never really felt like I was hypnotized. It just felt like I listened to those suggestions and relaxed, and that was enough. What I learned is that I didn't have to believe in it, I just had to do it.

Ilene

I had always imaged hypnosis as being some kind of dream-like state, in which I would be "out of it," unable to experience pain, extremely susceptible, and "waking up" with the snap of someone's fingers. I thought that someone else was going to "do it to me." Hypnosis was something I saw as weird, and unexplainable.

What I learned was how very rewarding and empowering the Leclaire method and hypnosis was for me: to be able to control my breathing, my consciousness — even my blood pressure! I was far more in control than I had imagined I would be.

During the pregnancy, hypnosis afforded me the opportunity to relax when I didn't have much time to spare (being the mother of a pre-schooler). For short periods of time I could feel relaxed, and then felt rejuvenated and able to take on the demands placed upon me in my personal and professional life. I was always amazed at how I was able to feel calm, truly relaxed and "centered."

I enjoyed the class with couples. My husband and I didn't practice much together, yet we really enjoyed sharing the experience with others, looking forward to the births of our babies. I found it really interesting that most of the participants were second-time mothers who wanted this particular birth to be different from their first.

A particular memory for me in class was the day we discussed pain, our fears, and how to manage them with hypnosis. When we did the exercise in which we were induced, and then had one of the men squeeze our ankles, I thought the men were only squeezing us lightly for fear of hurting someone. When we were brought back to our regular consciousness, and they squeezed our ankles again, I couldn't believe the difference. In front of everyone, I shouted, "I'm a believer!" (Previous to this, I was very skeptical about the way hypnosis would assist me in managing this pain for my child's birth. And yet, after we experienced this exercise, I was completely confident that this was going to work for me and my labour.)

I had a Caesarean section with my firstborn, and most of the experience was very scary, with needles and wires stuck inside my body. This time I wanted to feel more in control of the birth (well, as much as possible when you are a witness and participant in the miracle of life).

Experiencing labour the second time was totally different from my first experience. I could relax myself in between contractions, and also breathe through the pain in a different way. Yes, I still did experience pain, but it didn't appear to be as intense as with my first child.

I didn't need any medications, and the labour itself was very short. I was told that labour actually becomes quicker with hypnosis. I believe this to be true, because my body only dilated to four centimeters with my first child. And with this second birth, it was amazing to watch how quickly I progressed.

After Joshua was born, I felt exhilarated, feeling that I was able to "take on the world." In fact, we left the hospital the same day!

Whenever I tell people how wonderful the pregnancy and birth were, I ALWAYS mention that the Leclaire classes helped to make them that way. I feel that I've acquired a skill that will last me the rest of my life.

◈ Epilogue

Something we were withholding made us weak until we found it was ourselves.

Robert Frost

Many feelings arise with pregnancy. Perhaps the degree of pain is a direct correlate to all that is attached to the child, to the umbilical cord. Does the pain come from our trying to hold back? If we could unite with other women and with men and they with us, we could transform each other.

Jung speaks of the collective unconscious. Could there be a collective body memory? Women of all time have been birthing babies. Our bodies know exactly how to birth our babies, just as the earth knows how to give blossom to the flowers. It is easy. It is we who participate in making it difficult. You can change that by:

1. Trusting your body.
2. Quieting your mind.
3. Increasing your awareness of the myths.
4. Creating your own birthing plan.

There is no learning without memory. Give your mind a memory of a beautiful vaginal birthing, pain-free, fulfilling, letting go easily pushing your baby out. Imagine your body joining in a collective body memory. Choose a woman of long ago. Let her be your guide. She birthed many babies out in the open air in a beautiful field with flowers. She was at one with the fecundity of the earth. She opened the mouth of her womb as wide as petals in full bloom, making a passage for her children and your children. She gave birth as Mother Earth gives birth in a sacred moment, in touch with the wisdom of her own body and that of the earth. For one perfect moment, see yourself united.

◆ Index of Terms

Bibliography

Croce Benedetto, *Aesthetics*, Boston, Non Parei/Books 1983

Edinger Edward, *Ego and Archetype*, New York, Penguin Books 1986

Hawking Stephen W., *A Brief History of Time*, New York, Bantam Books 1988

Jaffe' Aniela, *The Myth of Meaning in the Work of C. Jung*, Zurich, Darmon 1984

Jung Carl G., *Dream Analysis*, edited by William Mc Guire, Princeton University Press 1984

Kushi Michio and Aveline, *Macrobiotic Pregnancy and Care of the Newborn*, Tokyo, Japan Publications 1983

Lamaze Fernand, *Painless Childbirth: the Lamaze Method*, Chicago, Henry-Reg Nery Company 1970

Leboyer Frederick, *Birth Without Violence*, New York, Alfred A. Knopf 1984

Loughlin Tom, *Jungian Psychology Vol II : Jungian theory and therapy*, Los Angeles, Panarion Press 1982

Read Grantly Dick, *Childbirth Wthout Fear*, New York, Harper and Row 1944

Von Franz Marie Louise, *Creation Myths*, Dallas, Spring Publications 1986

Warner Marina, *Alone of All Her Sex*, New York, Vantage Books 1983

Wells G.A., *The Origin of Language*, La Salle, Open Court 1987

Suggested Reading List

O'Neil Leclaire Michelle, PhD., *Better Birthing with Hypnosis*, New York, McGraw/Hill 2002.

Cohen Nancy Wainer and Esther Lois J., *Silent Knife: Caesarean Prevention and Vaginal Birth after Caesarean*, South Hadley, Mass Bergin and Garvey 1983

Gaskin Ina May, *Spiritual Midwifery*, Summertown 1993
To order send $17.95 to: The Book Publishing Co, P.O. #99, Summertown, TN 38483

Kitzinger Sheila, *The Complete Book of Pregnancy and Childbirth* (new edition), New York, Alfred A. Knopf 1990

Kitzinger Sheila, *The Crying Baby*, London, Penguin Books 1989

Kitzinger Sheila, *The Experience of Breastfeeding*, Middlesex, Penguin Books 1987

Kushi Michio and Aveline, *Macrobiotic Pregnancy and Care of the Newborn*, Tokyo, New York, Japan Publications 1983
To order call or write: Kushi Institute, Box 110, Brookline, MA 02147 (617) 7310564

O'Neill Leclaire Michelle, *Creative Childbirth*, Los Angeles, Papyrus 1993

O'Neill Leclaire Michelle, *Creative Childbirth Birthing and Beyond* tapes and workbook, Los Angeles, Papyrus 1993

Read Grantly Dick, *Childbirth Without Fear*, New York, Harper and Row 1944/87

Weed Susan S., *The Wise Woman Herbal Childbearing Year*, Woodstock, Ashtree Publishing. P.O. # 64, Woodstock, NY 12498

Michelle Leclaire O'Neill PhD R.N. is director of the Leclaire Birthing Center and is a pioneer in the study of mind-body integration for treating infertility and pre term labour.

Dr O'Neill is in private practice in Pacific Palisades, California and is on the staff of the Simonton Cancer Center.

Dr O'Neill is also author of the Birthing and Beyond tapes and workbook for pregnancy and birthing and the Meditation and Healing tape for herpes, cancer and HIV.

Leclaire Birthing Center provides education, prevention treatment, hypnosis, meditation training, support groups and home visits for pregnant mothers, infertility, vaginal birth after one or more caesarean sections and pre and post partum depression.

NOTES

See It Live on Film!

Now available
Leclaire Hypnobirthing—Pregnancy Class
Video Tape $12.95

For further information or to order (check, money order, Visa or MasterCard) please write:
Dr. Michelle Leclaire O'Neill
P.O. # 1086
Pacific Palisades, CA 90272
For telephone consultation or appointment please call:
(310) 454-0920
E-mail: birthing@gte.net
Web page: www.leclairemethod.com

Birthing and Beyond tapes and work sheets

Tape I- Side A- Hypnosis and Pregnancy
$9.95

Tape II- Side A- Hypnosis for Labour (Hypnolabor) (to be played during 39th week and as soon as you go into 1st stage of labour and throughout labour as needed). $9.95

Form for how to change your unhealthy beliefs and how to feel better fast $2.00

Guidelines for support person during labor $1.00

Music tape- Side A and B- Baroque Peaceful Baby
Largo movements for centering
Right and Left Brain- For relaxation, concentration and meditation during pregnancy, labour, birthing, breast feeding and sleepless nights $13.95

Creative Child Birth $11.95
All shipping is $6.00 (six U.S.A. dollars) for 1 lb. or under. We ship priority mail. If priority rate changes cost is priority rate plus 50¢.

Complete package $47.95

Meditation and Healing Tape
For nausea, herpes, stress, cancer and HIV $ 9.95